P9-DET-182

THE CARDINAL MÜLLER REPORT

Gerhard Cardinal Müller
Prefect of the Congregation for the Doctrine of the Faith

with

Father Carlos Granados

The Cardinal Müller Report

An Exclusive Interview on the State of the Church

Translated by Richard Goodyear

IGNATIUS PRESS   SAN FRANCISCO

MORRILL MEMORIAL LIBRARY
NORWOOD, MASS 02062

282.09
Muller

17.95

Original Spanish edition:
Informe sobre la esperanza: Diálogo con Carlos Granados
© 2016 Biblioteca de Autores Cristianos, Madrid

Cover photo: Cardinal Müller by Stefano Spaziani

Cover design by Roxanne Mei Lum

© 2017 by Ignatius Press, San Francisco
All rights reserved
ISBN 978-1-62164-148-3
Library of Congress Control Number 2016951956
Printed in the United States of America ⊗

CONTENTS

INTRODUCTION

Cardinal Müller's tone is direct and frank. He does not shrink from addressing the most sensitive questions. He might sometimes make a joke and then add, in a conciliatory tone: "We had better not include that in the interview." He does not at all fit the stereotype—formal, diplomatic, cold, calculating—of a member of the Curia. He sometimes takes his time in answering; a silence falls in which the interviewer considers asking another question. But it quickly becomes apparent that he is thinking. His conversation flows calmly and firmly. He knows from the beginning where he wants to end up. In addition to being the Prefect of the Congregation for the Doctrine of the Faith, Gerhard Ludwig Cardinal Müller is one of the most outstanding figures in theology today. As a theologian, he is a believer who strives to give God's answers to men's questions. As the Prefect of the Faith, he has a privileged perspective on the circumstances, the horizons, and the questions that open up before us.

But what questions do our contemporaries have? What answer do they demand from the believer? People today do not see their lack of faith as a tragedy, but what does worry them profoundly is their lack of hope, for which—making matters worse—they try to make up with substitutes like optimism. The key question, therefore, is one of hope. And our contemporaries wonder whether there is hope for the "now", they wonder whether they can find it in Christianity—and they wonder, above all: What is the foundation of Christian hope?

The interview with Cardinal Müller that follows this introduction took hope as its basic subject: it is a "report on hope". I do not want now to go into the topics that will be developed below, in the prefect's answers. I would like simply to describe here the genesis of this book and to identify some keys to an understanding of the order of the questions posed to the prefect.

I had the good fortune two years ago to prepare and publish in the BAC[1] a short interview with Cardinal Müller entitled *The Hope of the Family*. This was a brief conversation that covered a narrow subject and was aimed at illuminating and giving hope to families in the context of the Extraordinary Synod on the Family of 2014. Even then there was hovering in my mind the possibility of an interview that could help bring into focus the various questions that had become urgent in our Church. The subject of hope seemed in any case to be a promising point of departure. All that was needed was to broaden the framework of the questions and lay the groundwork for a more relaxed dialogue.

But, first and foremost, the prefect would have to join in this new effort. As soon as that first interview was published, I wrote to Cardinal Müller proposing now the preparation of a text that would cover substantive issues, to which he would have to dedicate, not just a few hours, but rather at least an entire weekend. To my surprise, the prefect welcomed this initiative, offering me his time and making himself available. We set the meeting, this time reserving more days for the work.

Preparing the questions was quite a research project. It required choosing the right subjects and essential issues and working out a structured set of questions that would serve

---

[1] *Biblioteca de Autores Cristianos*: Library of Christian Authors. – TRANS.

as the path and the compass of the conversation. In the end, the subject of hope provided the right key: What can we hope for from Christ? What can we hope for from the Church? What can we hope for from the family? What can we hope for from society? This series of four broad questions made for a fine framework in which to set the relevant concerns, the "joys and the hopes ... of the men of this age". The questions on the subject of mercy were added later, in the context of the Year of Mercy, as a perfect conclusion to the rest of the interview. Each of these broad issues later served to gather together detailed questions, the specific subjects that required clarification. With respect to the subject of the family, I think it is relevant to note that the book was finished at the beginning of March 2016, when we still did not have the text of the Apostolic Exhortation concerning the Synod on the Family, which Pope Francis was preparing.

And so, with tape recorder in hand and the "arsenal" of questions prepared and gathered in quite a few folios, I rang the intercom at the prefect's house one quiet Saturday morning early in December for the interview. What followed were two extremely intense days of work—not that they were devoid of humanity, humor, and relaxed (unrecorded) conversation during meals and breaks. Cardinal Müller speaks perfect Spanish. He was even able to joke in the language of Cervantes. He learned our language during his sojourns in Peru, and he later continued to practice and perfect it. The whole interview therefore unfolded in Spanish. A German-Spanish dictionary, the *Catechism of the Catholic Church*, and the Bible were the books we had on the table before us.

During those two days, the cardinal showed himself to be, in addition, an indefatigable worker and a warm host. He took pleasure in showing me the meticulously maintained and very complete library in his house. And he tackled the work with true tenacity. In the end, I had the easier part of it: to listen, to record, and to take a few notes here and there. The prefect had the hard part of the work, because the questions (as the reader will see) were neither superficial nor obvious.

Those two days bore their fruit in many hours of tape, which then had to be transcribed, reread, corrected, polished, and so on. Actually, the weekend was just the beginning of the months of work that followed. All of it was obviously done in sustained contact with the prefect, who followed it closely every step of the way, constantly reading and rereading the text, retouching, adding, and improving. The interviewer, who was no journalist, did not want (or perhaps know how) to embellish the text with rhetorical flourishes. It might have been a good idea to accommodate a more journalistic style, but I think the result respected all the more the tenor of the interview and its objective of going into the substance of the issues.

In conclusion, I would like just to touch on the main heading of this book. The reader will perhaps have noticed that the heading "A Report on Hope" recalls the famous book-interview, with the Spanish title of *Informe sobre la fe*,[2] that the then Prefect of the Faith, Joseph Ratzinger, granted to the journalist Vittorio Messori (a book published, incidentally also by the BAC, in 1985). The parallelism is certainly intended as a homage to the friendship between the current prefect and the pope emeritus; but it is also, and above all, intended to bring to bear the focus of that interview. In it, Ratzinger completely and accurately diagnosed the situation of the Church, its causes and its

---

[2] "A Report on Faith". Published in 1985 by Ignatius Press in English (translated by Salvator Attanasio) as *The Ratzinger Report*. – TRANS.

effects, and also proposed some paths to a solution. It can be said that ensuing events have validated his focus, which was the subject of so much argument at the time.

The heading "A Report on Hope" brings to the fore a new subject, because (as will be explained in the first questions) we are today living through a great crisis of hope. "I say with great sadness and concern that many of our contemporaries, brought up in a world without God, are not convinced that history—even their own personal history—has a story line: a beginning and an end. The past of the individual, the family, or the entire population itself is experienced as a series of unconnected bursts, little anecdotes that offer no more than meager hopes and do not constitute a noble story that elevates them, that gives meaning to their whole life, that explains why they are here, what they are living for, why they suffer ... so it inevitably ends in a crisis of hope."

This new diagnosis of the current situation implies, too, that we need to ask new questions. That is why this interview was urgently needed. The prefect's words fill us with a deep breath of hope; they help us understand that problems are also opportunities for growth and that, above all, they are part of the ministry, of God's plan as it continues, little by little, to be realized in history.

CARLOS GRANADOS
General Director, BAC

THE INTERVIEW

Therefore, since we are justified by faith, we have peace with God through our Lord Jesus Christ. . . . and hope does not disappoint us, because God's love has been poured into our hearts through the Holy Spirit who has been given to us.

(Rom 5:1, 5)

To Pope Francis,
who has bestowed on the Church
this Jubilee Year of Mercy
ANNO DOMINI 2016

A REPORT ON HOPE

"Please do not let yourselves be robbed of hope! Do not let hope be stolen! The hope that Jesus gives us." This exhortation by Pope Francis [in his March 24, 2013, homily in Saint Peter's Square] is a great call to us: an appeal to a hope that goes beyond naïve optimism, a hope rooted in a desire not to lose sight of our goal, the true, great hope that only Jesus can give us. But, first and foremost, what is Christian hope, what does it consist of, what does it mean?

Man is always striving toward the future, imagining it, planning for it, dreaming about it ... Life always holds the promise of the new and appealing, as we hope to find something different and great that will enable us to grow as a person. Yet the future is the realm of the unknown, too, and it harbors threats that awaken fear. Hope is precisely what enables us to move toward the future, placing our trust in the buds that are the harbingers of the plenty we long for and that, in addition, enable us to conquer our fears.

There are spheres of human life that engender what we can call "natural" hopes. Consider the experience of love, which always carries a promise of eternity and enables the lovers to imagine a future full of new possibilities. Or consider the child who, just by being born, opens new horizons to his parents and society, lengthening their perspective on the future.

But all these hopes, in themselves, fall short. If we are able to embrace them, it is because they already shine with the great hope to which Pope Francis is alluding in the exhortation you just quoted, and also Pope Emeritus Benedict in his encyclical *Spe salvi* (see no. 39). It is the hope of God, trusting that life can fulfill its purpose and conquer all fears, including that of death: this hope is like the gold nugget that glows in the bottom of the pan, as though it were a touchstone of our everyday hopes.

We could say that everything Jesus did was a work of hope. He was born as "the hope of Israel" (see Jer 17:13), and in his preaching he sowed hope in the paths of men, opening their eyes, enabling them to walk, freeing them of the sins that stood in their way ...

But we could also ask ourselves, how do we attain this future? Is it not too great and lofty for us? This is the key to what Jesus proposed: not only did he open the future to us, he also offered us the way to attain it. We find in Jesus' love a promise that gives us the capacity to hope above and beyond our strength. With Christ's support, we trust that he can guarantee the greater hope, the hope that goes beyond simple optimism. This true trust is no longer based on a mere positive calculation of what we can attain; it now takes its strength from God in Jesus, who is the guarantor of his great promise.

This is the true theological hope, because it takes its meaning (*logos*) from the goodness of God (*theos*). We therefore say that hope is a supernatural virtue, because it is fixed on God as the ultimate end of everything. Realistically, we seek support in God in order to attain the goal that we recognize as being the one for which we have been made and to which we have been called.

Christian hope, then, is the only one that can grant us the certainty we crave. God has a universal plan to save us, and he has realized it in his Son, Jesus. That hope allows us to rely on God as the absolute future, rather than on our own projects and plans, which are subject to so many limitations: this is the certainty that is fostered by hope.

Are we undergoing today a crisis of hope, of this great hope that moves us toward God? It seems as though man's problem today has to do with faith, but especially regarding the ability of faith to open up the future; it therefore seems, at bottom, to be a problem of hope. The various crises that dominate the present grow out of just that, an uncertainty about the future: the economic crisis, the crisis of safety in civil life (terrorism), the crisis of falling birthrates ... Is that right?

Hope and faith are inseparably joined to each other, and to love. The three theological virtues express the new life that Christ has given us or, what amounts to the same thing, the fresh, novel, and even transgressive way we relate to God and to reality as a whole.

In the Bible, these three virtues continually intertwine with and reinforce each other. The purpose of *faith* is to recognize God himself as the foundation of all reality: his existence, his acts of salvation in history, his ever-faithful company. *Hope* is directed to God in his goodness, his justice, his mercy, as the ultimate end toward which everything is oriented. Supernatural *love* is the intimate union of God with us: he lives in us, and we are his children.

Whoever we are, we want to be happy: we all want true love, full justice, everlasting beauty. If we hope to attain full happiness in God, it is because at some point in our lives we have seen and read our reality, and when we discover in it a desire for the infinite, we have said yes to the only way to sustain our desire. Sure of his fidelity, we have freely entrusted ourselves to the One who fully keeps his promises and loves us. The question about

God brings my historic freedom into play. In whom shall I ground my life? Who, for me, is God?

True hope is only possible if we ground our life in God, revealed as the Father, Son, and Holy Spirit; his nature as the Trinity reveals to us our own threefold nature, because we are able to recall that everything proceeds from the Father, to discover through our intellect our inherence in the Son, and to accept in the Spirit the loving relationship between the Father and the Son. In Christ, God approaches every one of us and shows us his face. If, when we see that he is the beginning and provident presence of history, we humbly confess to his Son, we will discover in ourselves the gift that enables us to live without fear: that gift is faith, that liberating and consoling certainty, that roots us in meaning, that enables us through love to hold fast to our present history, and that, by opening us to the future without the least fear, sustains our hope. Saint John of the Cross, the exponent of Christian mysticism, has sung as no one else has about the transformation of one's perspective on the world that is wrought on the loving soul by the grace of the beloved, the sublime, and the everyday:

> Spilling out unbounded graces
> Hurriedly he passed these groves;
> Fleetingly gazing,
> His glance alone
> Left them blanketed with beauty.
>
> — (*Spiritual Canticle* 5)[1]

The overflowing grandeur of this trinitarian understanding of man and history as being rooted in a God

---

[1] Translation by Fr. Bonaventure Sauer, O.C.D. – TRANS.

who gives us being, who treats us as his children, and who invites us to love the world passionately contrasts with the vision that our Western societies usually offer us. There is so much fear of the future to be seen in them! So many specific fears, and also undefined ones! So much fear hidden behind an idolatrous, ever-expanding cult of ideology, of sex, of image, of the nation! Strangely, reflexive reason—that modern utopian reason that dispensed with faith because it supposedly represented obscurantism and decrepitude—came to trust in unlimited progress and the irrational sentiment of this or that dictatorial will almost as though they were articles of faith. This new era in human history began as a movement of optimism and hope in a period called "the Enlightenment" that engendered the fears of today. The point was to open oneself to the future by overcoming the memory of the past, to reject tradition and remake history, to eschew all dogma and place the hope of humanity, absolutely, in the new possibilities promised by technical and scientific progress. With what have those promises left us?

Are they perhaps promises of happiness that, by renouncing God and grounding themselves solely in human progress, leave us glutted by worldly goods but empty of hope?

That is right, and I say with great sadness and concern that many of our contemporaries, brought up in a world without God, are not convinced that history—even their own personal history—has a story line: a beginning and an end. The past of the individual, the family, or the entire population itself is experienced as a series of unconnected bursts, little anecdotes that offer no more than meager hopes and do not constitute a noble story that elevates them, that gives meaning to their whole life, that explains why they are here, what they are living for, why they suffer ... so it inevitably ends in a crisis of hope.

In reality, by rejecting faith in God, by losing sight of his bountiful generosity and the blessings we have from him in our life—that is, by losing our foundational memory, forgetting that he is our beginning and foundation ... we have turned into little gods who refuse to reach deep into ourselves and who end up redefining our identity according to our whim. This Western culture that, taking erroneous philosophical and theological conceptions as its starting point, has come to see no need of God as the foundation of man and being has lost not only faith but also hope and, with it, excellence. In the words of David Goldman, the author of books such as *How Civilizations Die*, the banality of the West is discouraging.

Without God, we lose the courage to confront the great existential demands that inevitably arise in our lives: death, sickness, suffering, violence, and so on. We could avoid them in a thousand ways, but in our lucid moments we will discover that we are empty and lost. Only by looking upon the face of God, which reveals itself to us progressively and intimately in Christ (see Num 6:26), and trusting in his Providence will we receive the strength required to address decisive and ultimate questions. Faith, understood as the placement of our trust in him who has made the greatest of all promises, generates trust and therefore hope. Only a believer can truly hope.

But is it possible to relight the flame of hope once it has seemingly been extinguished in men's hearts?

We have here a great mission for the Church: to show that the life of faith is the wellspring of hope. Man today does not perceive his lack of faith as a tragedy, but, on the other hand, he is indeed profoundly worried about his lack of hope. And, what is worse, he tries to make up for it with substitutes, such as optimism.

We resort, sometimes a little shamefacedly, to obvious and absolutely superfluous "self-help dynamics" that are steeped in a vague optimism; we apply makeup not only to our faces but to our whole lives; we immerse ourselves again and again in the virtual worlds of televised fiction so we can "live" stories that always have a happy ending; we believe each and every message that the media throw at us about the benefits of our technologized society; we give full faith and credit to the electoral messages that promise us a paradise on earth, in exchange for "no more than" our vote (our will) and our refusal to hold politicians to an ethical exercise of power (our conscience). To be able to go on being optimists, . . . we pay a high price!

With the constant self-censorship we apply in order to avoid seeing the negative in life, we end up committing great violence against ourselves and, in the end, against those who try to "rain on our parade". How much skepticism and cynicism is generated by the very pervasive mindset of the optimist that is in fashion today! How much irrationality is hidden by the supposedly rational approach of this "new man" who, for example, looks on impassively at the dangerous demographic decline of the West and fails to decide to raise the fertility rate or adopt the responsible immigration policies that we need!

Where are there recognizable signs of hope?

Reason, when one lives in harmony with faith, is able to recognize "the hope that does not disappoint us" (see

Rom 5:5). Consider that, as Benedict XVI affirmed in Regensburg on September 12, 2006, our great Western civilization was born of the mutual interaction of four age-old movements: the questioning tradition of Greece, the prophetic Hebrew tradition, the Catholic faith, and modern freedom of conscience. According to that pope, the only possibility for contemporary man lies in taking the question of God as his point of departure and, from there, applying his entire capacity for reason.

The new humanism that we have to develop sees no contradiction between the quest of reason and the act of faith, because the latter confirms for us that God is love, and that he has acted concretely in the world, and especially in my life, thereby showing me his love. This new humanism that will not give up in its passionate search for truth enables me to live in hope. For that reason, we must affirm that the teachings of the Church and all her doctrine, with the help of faith, constitute a valid premise for man today, because they enable us to recognize the goal toward which we must strive and the forces on which we can rely to reach it.

In any case, only faith allows us to rediscover the many signs of hope that society offers. Although it is true that there are signs of despair, such as the selfishness that prevails again and again in the world's political and economic life, for example, or many people's lack of desire to have children, faith enables us to detect the elements that reinforce our hope: there are many men and women in the political and economic spheres who exert themselves in serving the common good, or, to continue with the previous example, we see many brave and stable young couples who want to have children and who then care for them responsibly, providing for their education and looking out for their future. Bringing a child into the world is precisely the image that acts as a powerful reminder that the hope that does not disappoint us is possible. Our awe at the birth of a child brings home to us that everything we are and do is rooted in a gift, a "thou" who has given us the gift of life expecting nothing in return; a great love has welcomed us into a family and watched over us constantly.

Does Christian hope always imply optimism in dealing with problems, a positive evaluation of things?

Living in hope does not rid us of the problems we have in life. That has always been so. Never in our history, since the original sin, has there been an "earthly paradise". Infant mortality, wars, slavery, the oppression of the poor … the history of the human race is witness to the age-old existence of these plagues. Human misery exists. Our frailty is real. Placing our hope in God therefore does not mean the elimination of suffering but, rather, opening it to a horizon of understanding that in any situation, however difficult and tragic it may be, there can be a fertility, a fruit, because suffering, having been shouldered once and for all by Christ, can awaken and ripen love.

I believe that our society of today, by seeing God as metaphysically superfluous and proposing an optimism that is not sustained by reality, is exacerbating even more the problems that afflict it. A skeptical and hedonistic way of life, so totally contrary to human nature, is becoming more and more widespread, damaging us irremediably. Look at the resignation that is now so pervasive and the despair of so many who cannot find meaning in life. If we add agnosticism to these as a common premise—that is, an invitation to avoid seeking out the ultimate truth of things—the landscape is bleak, because despair always brings with it the obfuscation of truth. I believe we should reflect more often on the fragility of so many of our contemporaries: immersed in a virtual reality and therefore bereft of hope, they have also lost the meaning that transcends finite creation and the certitude of which the love of God, manifested in his works, is the only possible source.

The root of these forms of nihilism in man today is a radical loss of self-respect. They have convinced man that he is nothing more than another stage in the evolution of the material world, the product of blind chance in the development of nature. They have persuaded him that all of reality is purely material and pan-natural. Benedict XVI has called attention to this crisis by declaring that man today rejects the idea that he was created, having received an essence that we know as human nature, and he therefore refuses to accept that his life originated as a gift. That is the reason he presumes to posit self-generation as the foundation of his existence or, what amounts to the same thing, an absolute capacity to "reinvent" and redefine himself.

Our society, which congratulates itself on the democratization of culture and information, nevertheless looks on impassively at the marginalization of intellectuals who propose hard truths, at the repeated appearance of beliefs that are irrational and insulting in their vulgarity, at the spread of destructive ideologies that impose themselves under a cloak of political correctness, at the secret maneuvers of a few, swollen with economic power, who manipulate at will the consciences of the great mass of the population. Having substituted secular thinking for the Christian religion, we are not even surprised by the general disrespect for philosophy and the humanities in our secondary and higher educational institutions and, even worse, the systematic persecution of the possibility of entrusting ourselves to a personal God in our consciences, proposing to replace him with idols that are much more indulgent of our vanity and mediocrity. In the end, the beneficiary is whoever holds a share of power, small or large, in our society, because man is made much more malleable by this process.

It is sad to have to render this diagnosis of an anguished world in its deep-rooted finitude and solitude. It pains me that I have to recognize that we theologians have also played a part in the reduction of God to a mere instrument of logic in the hands of philosophical reflection, forgetting that absolute love is what our being is founded on and what transforms history into the history of salvation. Yet, I would fail my conscience as a theologian if I, too, were to remain silent about the truth of what I find in the facts.

Precisely because of what we see in this landscape, would it not be more prudent to cut back our expectations, not to hope for too much from the future, to content ourselves with a more moderate and considered hope?

We cannot resign ourselves, we cannot say, "the times are what they are", "this is how we have to live", "this is the nature of our period in history", "there is nothing we can do", "secularism is our fate." It is precisely the characteristic of hope that, in order to attain its goal, it does not rely on its own strengths. Faith guarantees us that God's strength is always greater than human weakness and the attacks of evil. Hope does not disappoint us (Rom 5:3–5) and cannot be subdued by those who hold the reins of power; for that reason, it is ultimately seen by the world as a subversive element.

Instead, the great questions we have to ask ourselves, those of us who want to resist submitting to this relativist dictatorship, are these: What is my responsibility as the father or mother of my children? What ethics and morals do I want to teach them? What political principles should I support with my vote in order to work for the common good? Answering such questions involves explicitly spelling out the hope that is in us (see 1 Pet 3:15). This well-founded trust means, in the end, that the whole history of salvation leads to the ultimate good and that nothing that is good, beautiful, and true in our life will be in vain or go to waste.

When the great totalitarian ideologies failed, we fell into a new dictatorship: that of the dominant, monolithic, techno-scientific way of thinking and of consumerist individualism. Let me emphasize: our secularized societies are being dynamited from within by vulgarity and frivolity. Seized as I am with love for God and his creation, and having always sought an integral education (*paideia*) and explored deeply in the foundations that the Lord has laid in being and the behavior of man (*humanitas*), I am somewhat disconsolate here in the twilight of my life over the small amount of time devoted to study by many of our university students and over the lack of rigor in the theological education of so many clergy, to cite two examples. Why? I believe that once society fragmented into myriad individuals seen as *homo oeconomicus*, as just another number in the statistics of consumption, we resigned ourselves to aspiring to nothing more than a life of ease.

We justify evil, even, with the excuse that we are being realistic, forgetting that true realism is full of goodness, because it is born of the encounter between life and the truth: to be realistic is to immerse ourselves in reality, so let us not lose sight of the fact that the greatest reality that sustains everything is God. His plan of love and salvation for all of creation becomes a personal gift for each of us, offered in the life of Jesus, who accompanies us, sustains us, and gives us the ability to live in love. Christ is the truth and the light of the world and, therefore, the true expression of hope.

You just mentioned "light". It is a marvelous image of Christian hope. In the catacombs of Priscilla, there is the beautiful image of the star as a sign of hope: a lighthouse in the night. The first Christians encoded their hope in two icons: the anchor and the star. Pope Francis tells us: "The first Christians depicted hope as an anchor. Hope was an anchor fixed to the shore of the hereafter. Our life is precisely a journey toward this anchor." The anchor, transformed into the cross, became one of the great Christian symbols. Later, on the other hand, as we have said, the star— both the one that announced to the prophet Balaam the coming of the future Messiah and the one that guided the Magi toward Bethlehem—also became a crucial sign of Christian hope. Why these two icons of the anchor and the star? What experience do they represent?

The *star* is the *light* that shines in the night. Light is indeed the great symbol of hope, an element of the natural world that orients us and therefore has always had, both in everyday language and in philosophical parlance, a metaphorical sense: light for the eyes—that is, for the external senses, but also light for the inner senses, always via corporeality. A light that orients us, beyond simple physical orientation, vis-à-vis the ultimate meaning of life, of things, of the universe.

All of us have at some point recognized people who can orient us and act as reliable guides on the path of our existence. Sometimes, surprisingly, these guides are the simplest or most unsophisticated people, because "the Lord often reveals to the younger what is best" (Saint Benedict, *Regla* 3:3). We say of them that they are a light unto us, a photographic slide or transparency of him who is the "light of the world" (see Jn 8:12). Jesus has come into the world and with his love has saved and reoriented us: in thought and also in deed, especially when we have to make great moral decisions or answer to the yearnings for the infinite that we feel deep inside us.

The Son of God orients us toward an eternal life that reveals itself to us, here and now, as a seed. The then Cardinal Ratzinger, in his famous work titled *The Spirit of the Liturgy*, reminded us in 2000 of Saint Augustine's expression *Conversi ad Dominum*. He invoked it to emphasize that our liturgy, as befits the people of God on their journey, had to express fully this orientation toward Christ that comes out to meet us in order to satisfy our yearning for the infinite. The light of faith enables us to see it even now, as we can "see" the goodness, righteousness, truth, or love of a person. Looking beyond the veils of our limitations in this world, one day we will be able to see it face to face.

The other image you asked me to explain is the *anchor*. This piece of nautical gear expresses the certitude and conviction that are characteristic of Christian hope: God, in Christ, has not only decided to confer salvation upon us, he has also granted us that salvation already. That fact is symbolized by the "anchor of salvation", which is Christ himself. Thanks to it, we do not sail about aimlessly, buffeted by the waves and therefore condemned to failure: on the contrary, linked to Christ, we are assured of definitive victory.

The star symbolizes God as the end point of the road we are traveling. The anchor, for its part, symbolizes the God who supports us throughout our journey, sustaining us with his love: the anchor makes it possible for a ship to hold fast in the middle of the sea—that sea that, with its winds, with its dangers, with its storms, with its sometimes devastating power, is the symbol of our life. At one moment or another I say to myself, "I am happy, I have everything I desire", and the next thing I know, everything collapses and is lost. It takes only a few seconds for my whole life to change forever! This disquiet is very human, so we all yearn for a definitive security and stability. That yearning is an integral part of our existence.

Through faith, we know that this hope, so legitimate, can only be God. Teresa of Jesus, the saint of Ávila, whose quincentennial we have just celebrated in 2015, said, "Let nothing disturb you, let nothing frighten you, all things are passing away: God never changes. Patience obtains all things. Whoever has God lacks nothing; God alone suffices." This prayer is not an expression of the false triumphalism of someone who knows he is better off than those who live in doubt: it is an example of a psalm of wisdom, in which a Doctor of the Church expresses the solace with which a soul is favored when it experiences, entirely gratis, the believability of God. Thus Saint Teresa teaches us that we can always count on God and always place our trust in him. The Lord—the "sweet good Jesus" who entranced her in ecstasy on that Easter Sunday evening in 1571 when she heard the novice Isabel de Jesús singing the little stanza "Let my eyes see you"—was Saint Teresa's anchor, and all the more so just when she was plunged most deeply into a profound spiritual loneliness and an increasingly appalling lack of understanding on the part of her beloved Church.

The Christian God, the God whom the saintly Carmelite of Ávila discovered, is never the product of our fantasies or of the ideology of the day. Nor is he the mathematical variable of a mental figment or a simple abstraction.

Even less is he a hypothesis that tallies well with some system or other. This completely and deeply nonconformist woman—this "restless, roaming woman" who continues to captivate those who are steeped in modernity, such as the great Edith Stein—tells us that in the midst of our difficulties, even those that "seem [to have been] sent by God to test us in suffering" (*Foundations* 28:3), God is the mystery that we "undergo and taste", an immediately present reality, a friend who, in all simplicity and innocence, pretends just to be there for us to happen upon by passing chance (*Life* 65:1). Let us place our hope solely in him!

But does Christianity truly offer hope for the "now"? This is a key subject of great interest that I would like to address. We run the risk of interpreting hope as a "not yet". The theologian Oscar Cullmann's phrase, which describes the life of a Christian in the world as an "already but not yet", has become famous. But doesn't hope offer something more? Should we not amend the phrase to read, "already but there is still more"? So I repeat, does Christianity offer hope for the "now"?

Oscar Cullmann, a great Protestant theologian, expressed the tension between two realities. There is, on the one hand, salvation through Christ, which is unsurpassable because we cannot go farther than Christ: Jesus is the Alpha and Omega, God's full communication with and presence among us. And there is, on the other hand, the Second Coming that we are awaiting still, the full consummation, the definitive appearance. What we have now is a salvation *sub signo*. The sacraments are the gift of salvation in Christ and at the same time the veil that hides it. God is now present only in faith; we will see his presence at the end times.

I believe, however, that we can and should correct Cullmann's formulation. In this theologian's background, we recognize the Protestant doctrine of justification, the *simul iustus et peccator* (Luther, WA 56:269), which, applied to all mankind, means we are "just" and "sinful" at the same time and in the same sense. According to this Protestant interpretation, the present, the current becoming of the world and of man, would be a "not yet" that is always contaminated by sin.

On the other hand, what do we say as Catholics? We affirm that we *already* and *now* have, in the actual presence of the Eucharist, the totality, the entire reality of Christ: the same reality that awaits us completely in the other sacraments. Certainly, we carry this "totality" in earthen vessels (2 Cor 4:7–15), to express that it is not something we have earned by our merit. Therefore it is right and just that we should give thanks for this totality of salvation that has *already* been given us. Our understanding, as Catholics, of the sacramental presence made flesh among us is not Platonic, as though we were awaiting an ideal future and had to content ourselves with some simple signs foreshadowing it. No: in the sacraments, which are effectual signs of grace, the treasure, the totality, has already been given us. This is something radical and new.

Here we find the true basis of Christian realism. Christ, by his Incarnation, has transformed the foundations of life, has made possible here and now a new life that accords with the gospel. The gospel will never be just a beautiful ideal that we take as a goal of life, knowing that only a few will attain it. On the contrary, the gospel has been made flesh in the Church, has been converted into a concrete way of walking and living, and has fostered social practices, ways of working, of celebrating, of conducting social relationships, of expressing ourselves, of conducting family life, or living with an illness or misfortune, that make it possible to move forward in trust.

The vision of a hope focused exclusively on the hereafter could devolve into a certain neglect of the tasks and hopes proper to this world. This is one of the great accusations that have been made against Christianity in the modern age by such philosophers as L. Feuerbach in his 1841 book *The Essence of Christianity*. Let us recall, however, the parable of the talents (Mt 25:14–21): it reveals to us that each of us has his own task or mission in this world. God has given us certain gifts that in reality are his, in order that, by giving them ourselves in turn, we would have more. How beautiful the mathematics of God! This call or vocation from God is what is called "positive predestination", in that he makes us the actuators of our lives, relies on our merits, on our meritorious acts.

A Christian can never live in a breach between earthly reality and a world situated in "the hereafter". This static duality is destructive. We believe and live in a dynamic unity, in tension between the responsibilities of this world, which are very important for eternal life, and the life that fully and definitively goes on after death. It is God himself who embraces these two dimensions of hope: the present and the afterlife. The new creation will be the consummation of heaven and earth, of human history in its entirety, and of all individual things.

Saint Augustine of Hippo's doctrine on hope has been summarized this way: "A life without hope is sad, but it is sadder still to live with a hope that has no foundation." What is the foundation of hope?

Hope gives us more than a new, very elevated goal that we must struggle to reach. That was the logic of the Stoics.

They proposed a kind of "penance" that consisted of a mea culpa for not having been perfect and therefore of a program of continuous new challenges and new efforts. In fact, it was the regimen of a man who, alone and wretched in the full sense of the word, would fight endlessly to attain his personal perfection.

Hope, understood in the Christian sense, begins with the conviction that we rely on divine support to reach our goal. Even though we do not deserve it. Even though we may be fragile and deserve being denied that help. "Lord, you know everything; you know that I love you" (Jn 21:17): this affirmation by Saint Peter, knowing that the Lord was gazing at him mercifully, sums up his whole life and is also the expression of his trust in the One who has given his life for him.

God reveals himself not only as the destination to which the road is leading, but also as the road itself. He invites us to come to him, not because we can do so alone, in reliance on our own strength, but because he offers us his sustenance on the way. Christ, as Saint Augustine said, is at once the homeland and the path to the homeland: "The homeland is on high; the way is low. The homeland is the life of Christ; the way is the death of Christ. The homeland is the dwelling of Christ; the way is the suffering of Christ. He who rejects the way, why does he seek the homeland?"[2]

Christ is the basis of Christian hope. When he became man, Christ took on, to and in himself, all that is human, and he transformed it. His resurrected humanity has been the foundation of all our hope; from it we can live, from it we can already participate, from it springs the possibility

[2] St. Augustine, Tractate 28:5, in *Tractates on the Gospel of John 28–54*, trans. John W. Retig, Fathers of the Church (Washington, D.C.: Catholic Univ. of America Press, 2002), p. 7.

of our full transformation in him, while we are still making our way.

I believe that, in our dialogue with our very secularized world, we run the risk of presenting Christianity as being no more than a system of values, hiding its essence: hope in him who has conquered pain, sin, and death. It worries me when I sometimes hear that "a Christian always has hope" or that "a Christian always has faith." I do not think we should pull these great words away from their roots in the person, in their foundation. Instead, we should say that "a Christian always has the hope *of Christ*", that "a Christian always has faith in *God the Father, Son, and Holy Spirit*." Without the specific person of Christ, Christianity is reduced to a philosophy, to a vision of the world like any other, confining the decisive moment of mankind in a simple sociological fact. But for man, as a person, only a person will suffice: Christ is our hope, is the only mediator between the only God and the multitude of men. Only with Christ as the starting point can the other support we need be truly firm and enable us to realize our hope.

I

WHAT CAN WE HOPE FOR FROM CHRIST?

Your last answer invokes and puts forward the subject of Christ.
He presented himself as the one who brought precisely the hope of
Israel, in abundance. How is that hope related to Christian hope?
I would like to recall in that connection some statements by the
Grand Rabbi of Rome, Riccardo Di Segni, who was scandalized
because it had been affirmed in the Synod on the Family that
"with Christ's coming and his reconciling a fallen world through
his redemption, the period begun by Moses ended." Rabbi Di
Segni answered: "With a certain callousness in form and sub-
stance, the bishops come to us today, we who follow the Torah
of Moses, to say that we are in sin and our era has ended. How
difficult this dialogue is!" Did Christ bring the hope of Israel to
an end?

The history of Israel is the history of God's revelation. The
God who reveals himself is affirmed by Jews as the Creator of all men and, at the same time, as the author of the
choice made by the people of Israel. Their hope, the hope
of Israel, is based on the powerful acts of God, who has
watched over them, who has saved them, and who has in
addition promised them an even greater salvation. That
hope takes shape in several forms. So, for example, Jews
await a full presence of God in a new Temple and also the

coming of a Messiah who, born in the house of David, will bring God's full peace to the world. And, beyond that, the prophets proclaimed that this coming will transform man's heart, making it faithful to the covenant with God and capable of a new love toward him.

For our part, we Christians believe that all this centuries-long anticipation was unsurpassably consummated when the God of Israel sent his Son, who became flesh and was made man for us. The son who was promised to Israel generation after generation is at the same time the eternal Son of God. The full presence of God that Israel awaited has been realized in the resurrected body of Jesus, the definitive temple of God. As the Pontifical Biblical Commission declared some time ago, however, it cannot be said that the Jewish messianic expectation is in vain, "because it can become for us Christians a powerful stimulant to keep alive the eschatological dimension of our faith. Like them, we too live in expectation." Conscious that "the spiritual patrimony common to Christians and Jews is thus so great" (*Nostra aetate*, no. 4), we know that the new religion became a reality through the body of a man, Christ, through his offering of love so that the law would finally be engraved in the human heart, as the prophets anticipated. None of the ancient teaching has been discarded: it has all been saved in the light of an extraordinarily abundant fullness.

It is the person of Jesus, then, who is the criterion for distinguishing Judaism from Christianity. They are two different religions. And yet we must deepen the inter-religious dialogue that we as Catholics are called upon to maintain with our Jewish brothers and that has found magnificent expression both on our part, for example in the text *Nostra aetate*, just quoted, and on the part of Judaism, with the statement *Dabru emet*, published in the year 2000 by 220 rabbis and intellectuals representing all the branches of Judaism. This dialogue deals mainly with theological questions, in addition to detailed political questions and cultural issues.

In the XIV Ordinary General Assembly of the Synod of Bishops, held from October 4 to October 25, 2015, commonly known as the "Synod on the Family", no bishop said that divine law or the Decalogue or the prayer of God's people or the Psalms or the presence of the Word of God that we find in all the books of the Hebrew Bible had been abolished or superseded. In fact, Christians value the law very highly: this is a gift of God to the people of Israel and to the people of the New Covenant, a light that enables our works. Certainly, any proposal to eliminate the law from Christian life or to regard it as an excessive burden would constitute a serious offense to Jews and would be especially an attack on the truth of Christianity.

The law, then, does not disappear in the presence of faith in Jesus but is, rather, reinterpreted in the light of the all-embracing law, the law of love, as Saint Paul said (see Rom 13:8–10). When the synod says that the period begun by Moses has ended, it must be interpreted, not as disrespect for the law, but as no more than a statement that it has attained its fulfillment. Jesus, in what is called the "Moses exception clause", affirming that "For your hardness of heart Moses allowed you.... [But] I say to you" (Mt 19:8–9), harks back to the words of the Creator, acts as a true interpreter of the divine will as revealed in the Word of God. That exception clause no longer has any meaning, because Jesus, overcoming hardness of heart, has established a new people among whom it is possible to live the goodness of the beginning of creation. The Church, as a body and as a people, in her complete visibility, in her social presence, in her institutions, in her discipline, can only reflect the new order instituted by Jesus that has superseded hardness of heart.

We Christians recognize, respect, and esteem our Jewish roots. In Saint John Paul II's historic visit to the Synagogue of Rome, on April 13, 1986, he referred to them as "our favorite brothers, and in a way our older brothers". Pope Benedict XVI, for his part, when he published the second part of *Jesus of Nazareth*, made a notable exegetic effort to explain some of the passages of the Gospel according to Matthew that have contributed the most to straining our relations with Jews. Finally, in July 2015, Pope Francis affirmed that the two communities have insisted on "a definitive 'yes' to the Jewish roots of Christianity and an irrevocable 'no' to anti-Semitism". A few weeks later, on September 25, 2015, this same pontiff, praying at the Jesuit Saint Joseph's University, in Philadelphia, and blessing there the statue *Synagoga and Ecclesia in Our Time*, moved us all when he highlighted the "voyage of friendship" that Jews and Catholics have undertaken since 1965 with the declaration *Nostra aetate* of the Second Vatican Council. In that regard, I believe that Francis' singular way of approaching this subject should be taken into account, because of his well-known personal friendship, dating from his years as the archbishop of Buenos Aires and continuing into his papacy, with prominent Jews like Rabbi Abraham Skorka, the rector of the Latin American Rabbinical Seminary in that city. The empathy radiated in Francis' meetings and the powerful images of his fraternal embraces clearly affirm that we share not only some values and historical recollections with Jews, but also the same God of the history of the salvation of the same chosen people. The God in whom we place our hope as Christian believers is the same God in whom Jews place theirs, to whom they pray and entrust their whole lives.

In fact, Christ's deepest secret is his Father, to whom he referred everything. The modern age has rejected the paternal image of God, trying to free itself from tradition in order to be able to generate a new hope in the future. But it seems that Jesus anchors his hope precisely in the revelation of the beginning, in the person of the Father. Can we say that the hope and liberation that Jesus brings us are his hope in the Father? What can we expect from the Father, just now in a time of crisis in paternity?

We must start by saying that Christ himself lived his hope in the Father. Christ expected a great deal from the Father. His whole life consisted in his union with the Father, in obedience to the plan of salvation that the Father had projected. What Christ hoped, first, was that the Father would bring to fullness the humanity that he had assumed: he hoped that the Father would glorify him with a glory appropriate to the Son of God. In his hope for himself, he also hoped for us, because the humanness that he had assumed was our humanness, our own flesh, thereby uniting himself in some fashion with every man (see *Gaudium et spes*, no. 22). Jesus hoped the Father would save the world from sin and fill it with eternal life.

Our vocation consists precisely of participating, in all aspects of our life, in the filiation of the Son. Every man and every woman are the objects of God's eternal love. After man fell into sin, the Son of God wanted, out of love, to enter this sinful world, this world of despair, of despotic domination and elimination of the weakest. God came into this world dominated by evil and pride, oppressed by the Prince of this world, as we read in the great prologues to the Gospel of Saint John, Colossians, Ephesians, or also in the hymn of the Letter to the Philippians. The Eternal made himself present in the temporal, the Infinite in the finite, to raise up the temporal and the finite to the rank of an eternal interpersonal relationship with God. In that fashion, he who was a slave recovered his dignity as a son. This daring anthropology, founded on the mystery of the redemption, expresses the concomitance of the hope of Jesus with the liberation of men ...

Apropos of this important subject of "liberation" that you just mentioned—if you will allow me the digression—what is your assessment of so-called "liberation theology"?

Lately the Magisterium has criticized only some of the elements of liberation theology. Specifically, it has criticized socio-analytic mediation and the partial use of Marxist conceptual tools, which are radically contrary to Christian anthropology. But it has considered other elements to be worthy of being taken into account, and even indispensable, such as the need to conduct an empirical and scientific-social analysis of the existence and reality of man that avoids the dualistic dilemma of the here and now as opposed to the hereafter. As I said in my book *On the Side of the Poor: The Theology of Liberation*, the postulates of this theology about the lack of any vague coincidence between earthly happiness and eternal salvation, considering history as a dramatic struggle between the dialectical forces of grace and freedom, on the one hand, and of sin and oppression on the other, can be correctly understood with the help of certain elements of the *nouvelle théologie*, studied in depth by my great friend the theologian Gustavo Gutiérrez (I see his theological development as a *nouvelle théologie* oriented to the social) or of the debate on grace that Karl Rahner championed (with a historico-social application).

Freedom, when it is understood from a Christian perspective, unlike that proposed by certain philosophers, has as its purpose not only the choice among certain or many possibilities; its essence is the power to choose the good as such, above all God the Father, the source of all that is good. To be free implies an ability to identify ourselves with God, finding the meaning of our life in our communion with him. Hope in Jesus, therefore, includes our freely given reply. God sees us, not only as objects for his action, but also as authentic subjects, protagonists of our salvation. We participate in the personal relationship between Father and Son, and he considers us his children and calls us to friendship with him. Faith roots us in a hope that does not disappoint: this is what Christ expected of the Father, and this is the hope that the Father fulfilled when he resurrected his Son.

In his interaction with the young people of Brazil, Pope Francis introduced himself this way: "I am not bringing gold or silver, but Jesus Christ." This is certainly our great hope: Christ. He gives us the seed of immortality and sets in motion within us, by the action of the Holy Spirit, the process of divinization, of transfiguration of our body into the image of his body. This is our hope. But is it not somewhat pretentious to think that our body can be transformed into the image of his by the action of the Spirit?

It would certainly be pretentious if it were our invention or projection. But we observe that Scripture attests to the transformation, into the divine, of the believer baptized in the humanity of Jesus, as a gift from him. A Christian does not place too much trust in the greatness of man but instead gratefully recognizes the grandeur of God, his generosity and his communicative capacity.

The great richness that Pope Francis tells us about is our incorporation into Christ, his having made us one body with him. As members of the Church, we have been linked to her in a visible corporeal connection. We are not part of a political party or a human organization but, instead, through baptism, are members of a living body and participate in the same life principle, the love of God. As Saint Paul says, "But when the time had fully come, God sent forth his Son, born of woman, born under the law, to redeem those who were under the law, so that we might receive adoption as sons" (Gal 4:4–5). Our wealth is our intimate communion with God: he is in us and we in him. We become God because we love what God loves. We are what we love.

The key to understanding this transformation into the divine, effected in us and solemnly proclaimed in Preface III of the Nativity of the Lord, is therefore love. Saint Irenaeus of Lyon was the first Father to formulate explicitly that God became man so that man would become God (see *Adversus Haereses* 19:1). Other Latin Fathers would do so later, like Saint Augustine (see *Sermon* 185) or Saint Leo the Great when he sang the Nativity of the Lord (see *Sermon* 26:6). But it was Clement of Alexandria who was the first to use the concept of man's transformation into the divine (see *Prot.* XI, 114:4). The Incarnation of the Son of God, therefore, is the cause of our divinization, while the Resurrection is what introduces this radical change in humanity.

Do these theological truths correspond to our experience? I believe that anyone can attest that all authentically human love involves participation in the other: when I love, I become one with the other person and I say to him, "You are in me." Love is much more than a relationship between two totally independent beings. In authentic love, we discover that our life is transformed and leaves behind its isolation to unite itself with the life of the beloved. We discover ourselves in a deep-rooted dependence on the other: a positive, creative dependence that enriches our life, that empowers the best in us and helps us overcome what makes us feel ashamed. We discover, even, that we are not the source of love but, rather, that it has been bestowed on us gratis, even undeservedly. Yes: the greatest discovery that any person can make is that of an authentic love, because it enables him, in turn, to discover God the Father, the origin of all and the foundation of our lives, whom his Son, Jesus, came to reveal. Love of this good Father encompasses all the dimensions of our life: it is spiritual, like light and strength, but also corporeal.

This transformation into the divine that we experience when we love and are loved is an "admirable exchange" (Saint Irenaeus, *Adversus Haereses* V, 8:1) because it never nullifies our humanity. On the contrary, in our consumerist, ideologized world, we will be obliged to declare tenaciously, even to the point of martyrdom, that man's great treasure and great hope is for human nature to be always open to the possibility of being penetrated and transformed by the transcendence of God's love.

To speak of the love that is poured out onto the Church is to speak of the Holy Spirit. We could say that Jesus fulfilled the hope of his followers through the gift of the Spirit. The gift of the Spirit is the culmination of all hope. In that sense, Pope Francis reminds us that the fundamental duty of the follower of Christ is "not to impede the Spirit". What hope does the Holy Spirit hold for us?

Without the Holy Spirit to enlighten us and give us strength, it would not be possible to go beyond the nihilism that we see in modern culture and civilization, in which we give priority to the marketplace and a life of ease. Without the Holy Spirit, we would be overwhelmed by our civilization, so worshipful of the privileged and powerful, the beautiful, the healthy. The Holy Spirit opens our eyes so we can see the man who is suffering—who is suffering physically and spiritually. The Holy Spirit enables us even to look at ourselves with mercy, because he is himself the expression of God's love. The Holy Spirit reveals to us how God acts.

We tend to seek out those who are in some way or other important to us, who entertain us with their conversation, whose character we find appealing, who will solve a problem for us in the future: they say here in Italy that if your friends include a judge, a doctor, and a priest, you have it made! God, on the other hand, goes in search of those who do not count in this world and loves them so much as even to give his life for them, not as mere objects that are separate from him, but as participants in his own being. He loves them with the love that he himself is.

It is therefore the Holy Spirit who introduces us into this marvelous loving relationship. Infusing his love in our hearts, he enables us to see the other with the eyes of God: he elicits a surge of compassion in us, the passion of the love of God. He enables us also to go beyond the limits of conditional love, because we also continuously experience that our love is very limited. He empowers us, especially, to participate in the same inner quality of divine love, the communion of three Divine Persons.

The personal relationship with God reveals us as both lovable and beloved. It helps us overcome our reductive vision, which is today very widespread and purports to subject us to the mere caprice of nature or a blind evolution. This relationship, however, restores us, because through the Spirit we can see man in his true fullness—that is, as a being who is the object of God's love and a participant in his own being, his love.

With the current resurgence of new forms of gnosticism, we Christians firmly declare that the Spirit of God is not "intellectual", is not of the mind as opposed to the body. We know from Scripture that the Spirit of God introduces us into the relationship of love with him and signifies it: in fact, he embraces all the dimensions of our life, including also our body, because through him we relate to the world and to other people. From the Spirit we hope, precisely, that he will little by little transform our whole concrete, corporeal, emotional, intellectual, and spiritual existence, to place it all at the service of love. Through the Spirit's presence in us, we can recognize that the consummation of our journey will be communion with God in our resurrected flesh.

In saying that the Spirit also transforms our flesh, you have touched on an aspect of the Christian vision of man that today, seemingly, we do not understand very well: Of what importance is the body for the fulfillment of man? Greeks, Jews, Romans ... they have each conceived of the body in their own particular way: Is it a prison? Is it pure weakness? In the framework of a society like ours, in which more and more behavior, paradoxically, is being generated in what has come to be called the "cult of the body", what is the significance to us of existing in a body? Can we hope for something for the body?

Certainly today's culture displays a great interest in the body—even in the degeneracy reflected in the "cult of the body" that is so widespread today and that a Christian should reject outright because, deep down, it hides a crass materialism.

To confront this very subtle temptation effectively, because we are bombarded continually, all day long, by more and more aggressive advertising against modesty and the most basic ethical rules, we would have to study more carefully the history of mankind and, specifically, the evolution over time of the conception of the human body.

You mentioned the Greeks. They understood that there was a mystery to the body, so they used it as a favorite object of art, especially in sculpture. But, at the same time, they considered only the healthy, beautiful body, full of life. What place in their conception was there for the suffering body, the body of the slave, the body of the mutilated, the diseased? I think they created a kind of abstraction of the body without understanding all of its experiences and dimensions, especially those of pain and frailty.

The tendency today toward the "cult of the body" drinks directly from this fountain, but in an exponentially exaggerated way. We forget quite easily that the body, harboring an impulse toward the divine, is called to express something beyond itself. This lapse is traceable to the antihumanist ideologies of the twentieth century. In the Congregation for the Doctrine of the Faith over which I preside, we have many documents, some of which are on permanent display in our archive, that attest to the fact that the Fascist and Nazi conception of the body had biologism and racism hidden within it. Something similar happened in Communism, another expression of totalitarianism: all these ideologies educated children and adolescents with a focus on a healthy body because, in reality, they had to be able to count on mothers who would breed new and hardy soldiers, who would in turn impose the madness of the political ideas they had developed in the laboratory of power. I would like also to emphasize that these three ideologies are the fruit of a modern society that turned its back on God, in which we ourselves live. It therefore should not surprise us that in the current fragmentary logic of propaganda and the mass media that sustain the market-place, the body should be considered as nothing more than a simple object of commerce and consumption.

To understand the body well, we have to recognize God as Creator and man as creature. Let us focus on Christian art: the representation of the bodies of Adam and Eve is the model for all that God has created; they are beautiful bodies because Adam and Eve are themselves good, because they express the fact that what God made is good, that we proceed from him and he has made us good. At the same time, however, Christianity does not forget suffering and pain: among the images most charac-teristic of Christian art, we also find the crucified one, full of wounds and deformed, or the sick, in the first represen-tation of the body lacerated by pain in some of the Roman sarcophagi depicting the miracles of Jesus. In these prim-itive representations of the Christian mystery, bodily pain shows us a path to the recognition of God's redemptive love. The third representation characteristic of this new Christianity is that of the resurrected body, full of the glory and love of God: its message is that God does not deprecate the body but, instead, fills it completely with life, linking the hope of man to his corporeal dimension. The depiction of the risen Christ was a representation of the future and end of man.

These three images in Christian art of Adam and Eve, Christ crucified, and the risen Lord offer us the key to an explanation of our body. The three stages in the history of salvation and, therefore, of the realization of man—that is, the creation, the redemption, and the glorification—express a true anthropology of the body. Man, the favorite creature of creation, has the capacity to distance himself

from God through sin: the crucified body of Jesus is the
culmination of this dynamic of death and break in communion. His glorified body, however, expresses the
dynamic of love that regenerates everything. Recognizing
these three moments, today's man can also be capable of
opening a path of hope for the body, for what he feels and
desires within himself.

The dogma of the Assumption of Mary's body also
explains this powerful truth. This mystery speaks in itself
only of what is most human and real: it is perhaps for that
reason that it has been so tenderly preserved in the popular devotion of the simple people and so harshly attacked
by certain theologians and intellectuals who, errone-
ously, consider it to be a myth or idea that will never
be realized. The Assumption of Mary, who is human
like us, explains the ultimate reality to which we all gain
access through faith, through hope, and through love—
that is, by partaking of the glory of the resurrected body
of Christ. In fact, it opens us to authentic reality—not
to the substitute that certain ideologies sell us—because
it reveals to us that our existence, here and now, already
demands the new and definitive garb that Christ will
grant us when we clothe ourselves definitively in him
"who will change our lowly body to be like his glorious
body" (Phil 3:21). It is for that reason that the sacrament
of baptism is so important: it initiates us symbolically
into the concrete participation in Christ crucified, dead,
and buried, announcing thereby that life is death with
Christ so as to be resurrected with him (see *Catechism of
the Catholic Church*, no. 1005).

*Contemporary phenomenology has presented the body as the
medium through which the person is present in the world and*

makes himself present to other men. How would this statement read in Christian language?

The body is what situates us in the world: it is not some accident but, rather, that which enables us to touch the most profound depths of our identity. Man can say, in a way, "I am my body", and, in consequence, "I am my relationships." We are the love that we receive and the love that we are capable of giving. It defines for us an encounter and a belonging. We participate in the world in the first person, in its spatio-temporal dimension of extension, of materiality, of events, of contact with other existing beings.

Therefore, history is conditioned on corporeality. Angels do not have a history, do not have a society, do not have a culture that grows and matures, do not have evolving ideas, do not deepen or increase their love. In contrast, we have a world in common, are part of a whole, and also realize the whole in its consummation. When he assumed our flesh, the Son of God came definitively into history, made himself one of us, became our brother, and enabled us to participate in his filial relationship with God.

God has loved more than just our soul. Saint John tells us that God loved the world (see Jn 3:16) in the sense of the whole of creation, of all that is developing toward its filial consummation. This reflection produces great consolation and great peace, because nothing that exists in history is forgotten by God: in fact, it is we who have a tendency to forget easily. The powerful of every age, no matter how many monuments they may erect to preserve their memory, know that time will take it upon itself to destroy and erase every trace of them.

Crossing Saint Peter's Square, for example, I notice the attempt of so many tourists to immortalize the moment of their visit to the Vatican and preserve it for history, without taking into account the fragility of our memory and the technical vulnerability of the photographic medium. I sometimes think that, instead of wasting that precious time taking dozens and dozens of snapshots that they will perhaps never look at again, they would make better use of it by walking calmly through the wonder that is Bernini's colonnade or enjoying the esthetic pleasure of looking at the always surprising cupola by Michelangelo. For God, everything is an eternal present; God has it all in his memory and, through the Spirit, loves everything in his Son. To learn to live in the present is to enter into God's time. Everything is present for him. Jesus, our Savior, is the great recapitulation of everything: everything has been created in him, and everything will be gathered up by him. Nothing will be excluded except evil, which is the contradiction of the totality of God's love.

Should this idea of the recapitulation of everything that is human in Christ spur a new esteem for man?

I believe, indeed, that nihilism, the great temptation of postmodern, technico-functional man, can only be defeated with a new hope and a new esteem for man.

When I experience my existence as though it were a falling leaf being wafted here and there by the passing wind, I fall into the error of functioning only by my senses, according to the logic of what is in my interest or to my advantage or, at most, according to a natural altruism. My hope is dramatically reduced. I thus diminish my human dimension to nothing more than nature: although what is natural is good, I should never give up searching for the ultimate foundations of existence. I cannot deduce the meaning of my life from the limited, finite, natural ends that this world offers me: if the "all" that it offers me has no meaning, neither do any of its parts. Without an infinite ultimate foundation, limited ends rest on emptiness and nothingness. In that regard, I believe the growing aggressiveness that we see in our Western societies is attributable, in good part, to the skepticism in which we live.

None of our acts have any meaning unless the whole has a universal meaning. If a great ship is sinking, what good does it do me to have a very comfortable bunk? We need to be able to find meaning in the whole, which can happen only if we accept and trust in God. Only God returns self-esteem and self-appreciation to man. Indeed, if my life proceeds from love, it contains a call to live in harmony with that love. Accepting God, I also accept the greatness of my actions and what I have at stake in them. As Romano Guardini pointed out, we must recognize the importance of the act of accepting ourselves: this free act enables us to recognize that we have our origin in God's love and that we receive our filial condition from him. "I have been situated in Being", Guardini says, in his work *Virtue, Issues and Insights into Moral Life*. That point of departure opens a new horizon of hope.

Is it, perhaps, that speaking of God does not sound very modern to many people or does not fit with the logic of a certain "intellectuality"?

God is seen as something for unthinking people who adopt a primitive, medieval outlook. A believer's way of thinking is seen as lacking the seriousness and rigor of atheism or, better still for some people, the more neutral and seemingly more honest mind-set of agnosticism. At times, it seems to me that some people make an effort to share questions with the believer and doubts with the atheist. That is a very comfortable position, as though allowing them to say at the Last Judgment: "We tried to be close to you, God, we called out to you, we strove, we have never done anything against the Church or Christianity, but we just could not get past our doubts."

This comfortable stance of uncertainty, indulged or fostered in man today, is not compatible with the word of Jesus. It is true that confessing that one is a believing Christian is not easy. There is persecution. It is understandable, too, that it engenders fear. But Christ never promised that the path of Christianity would be an easy way to attain popularity and applause. The question of the existence of God can only be answered, in the end, by one's own way of life, by no half-measures: we either affirm the existence of God in the way we live our own lives, or we live as though God did not exist—and so everything is permitted, as Dostoevsky said in *The Brothers Karamazov*. Man thereby gives up the search for God as the ultimate purpose of human life.

Paradoxically, some believers make it a habit to take an unflagging attitude of criticism toward the Church. They present themselves as having the same view as agnostics but simultaneously demand to participate fully in the life of the Church. The Bible offers a few examples of this attitude. The clearest one is Peter, who publicly denied the Lord: "Man, I do not know what you are saying" (Lk 22:60). We sometimes say the same about Christ and the Church: "I do not know them." This may be a part of the reason for the failure of our Catholic thought: the fear of confessing our faith. Faced with such an aggressively secular world, however, we cannot be afraid to present ourselves as convinced and practicing Christians! We cannot deceive ourselves with the idea that respect for the public square requires us to live our faith in private! We should never assume that building a pluralistic, tolerant, and respectful society entails silencing our faith and renouncing our mission, which is falsely identified with proselytism! Such behavior ill serves those who honestly seek the truth: true solidarity with non-believers requires explicitly offering them the truth, thereby giving them reason to hope.

What you have said reveals some risks of misinterpreting the hope that Christ brings us. There is a risk of falling into a gnostic approach, in which what we do does not touch man in the flesh. Pope Francis warned us about this risk: gnostic Christians dwell in the realm of ideas, with a diffuse and fluid faith. Another risk is that of the purely social approach, in which Christian action does touch real life, but it does so without opening it up to the Spirit, clipping the wings of hope. At the same time, there is the danger of a purely eschatological approach, which reserves hope for the hereafter, with no implications for the present. Do we live in the shadow of these risks? Where do you see them manifested?

The temptation to change or falsify the all-embracing character of Christianity and reduce it to a construction of our minds, a power structure overarching created reality, has always been present among believers. All too easily, they have forgotten the concreteness and facticity of Christianity.

Gnosticism existed in a specific historic form that was described very well by Saint Irenaeus of Lyon in his work *Adversus Haereses*, but it is also an abiding threat within Christianity. We could say today that gnosticism is revived in a vision of the person that concentrates on the subjective, the individual, and the interior and that considers everything that is corporeal or exterior as secondary. Irenaeus, on the other hand, saw with crystal clarity that the presence of God is alive in the concrete: the body permits relationships among individuals, the Church is visible, the formulas of faith express a life founded in God. For Christianity, all of this is not a mere outer or temporary garment but, rather, the concrete way in which the core Christian fact—the Incarnation of the Son of God, his death, and his Resurrection—is communicated to us. The Christian experience always begins with a personal encounter with Christ, who has been made flesh and existed in the world. The hope he brings us is not some distant ideal toward which we are moving but which is always unattainable. It is instead a concrete gift, realizable here and now, which enables us to live according to the teachings of Jesus.

Sociology has proposed to reduce religion to a social role. It has thereby thrown one aspect of the truth into relief: when a society is religious, it is characterized by a greater cohesion among men, producing a new unity among the different elements of the common good and a greater sensitivity to suffering. That is the reason that many of our societies tolerate (*sic*) the fact of religion, as long as it is subject to the limits set by the powers that be. That social utility, however, radically diminishes the religious experience, using it as a tool in the service of mundane ends. When the Church becomes just another social agency and is even seen that way by her members, who abdicate the exercise of her prophetic dimension, she soon loses all interest for people and comes to resemble salt that is thrown out and trodden under foot by men (see Mt 5:13).

In contrast, true faith is always searching for a greater hope, because it holds our mind and life open to the infinitude of God, who has risen above the mundane. As for the last risk you mention, I believe it should be emphasized to

present in the Church. We may not realize it, but it is always lying in wait.

I recall here a young man who said during confession: "I accept the sacrament of penance, but it seems a little ridiculous that I have to kneel here in front of you to confess my sins. It is not particularly a problem for me at the intellectual level, but it is not easy for me to get past this act of humiliation." I learned later that it was possible to enter into a dialogue with this young man, because he realized that God was not imposing on his life but instead giving simple signs that raised questions in him. This youth had been capable of formulating those questions with great honesty and then had also been capable of humbly accepting my answers.

You mentioned the sacraments as the means by which Jesus enters our life through simple signs. Can you develop this point a bit more?

Jesus wanted water to be used in the initiation of the faithful into the Church through baptism. That is, to produce in us an eternal effect, he did not want to rely on lofty speeches or mysterious words, but turned instead to the simple sign of water. It is through this divine medium, which is so simple and has its origin in the Incarnation and the Cross, that he makes us children of God. As Saint Paul found when he announced the Cross of the Lord, some people see it as a scandal, and others see it as folly (see 1 Cor 1:18–23), because where there seems to be nothing but irrelevance, failure, pain, and defeat for a life that is structured by rational logic, it is precisely there that God's limitless love is, which can save the lives of all. That is where the universality of redemption manifests itself, expressing the subjective character of the redemption. And that universal redemption includes my own, for Christ died also for me.

Only faith initiates us into authentic wisdom: if we recognize this definitive proof of God's love, if we find our strength in the humility of love and our wisdom in the weakness of renunciation, we are capable of leaving behind a life lived for ourselves. This is the "gospel of grace", which reveals to us that our salvation springs from Christ's death and not from our own strength or merit.

How much beauty and wisdom there is in the parable of the good Samaritan (see Lk 10:25–37), who was despised and considered by many to be a foreigner (see Jn 4:9; Lk 17:12–19)! When he approached the Jew who had been stripped and beaten, wounded badly, and left half dead, he did not make any grand declarations or great speeches. He surely did not know about the law or social distinctions. The love that beat in his heart manifested itself, not in lofty forms of address, but in acts (seeing, feeling pity, approaching him, bandaging his wounds, taking him to an inn, caring for him, paying the expenses), which are in some ways parallel to the reaction of the father of the prodigal son (seeing him from afar, being moved, running toward him, embracing him and kissing him, holding a feast for him: Lk 15:11–32). The Samaritan saw only that his neighbor was in need. With God's own heart, he forgot the disdain with which he had been treated in the past by true Jews, he humiliated himself, he gave himself over to his neighbor and treated him with mercy. This is love; God so loved the world that he gave his own Son so that we might all have life through our faith in Jesus Christ. This is the humbling of God, hymned by Saint Paul in his letter to the Philippians (see Phil 2:7).

It is useful to recall here Saint Gregory Nazianzen's reply to the heresy of Apollinaris. The latter said that Christ had not assumed a rational mind. Gregory answered him in the light of the mystery of salvation, asserting in a quotation that has often been attributed to Saint Irenaeus: "What has not been assumed has not been healed" (*Ep.* 101:32, *SC* 208:50). This means that God saves us in our existence, with our corporeality as the point of departure. He saves us in this state. He does not save us *from* the body but *in* the body, in our flesh, in tangible, material realities. That is why Pope Francis always insists on the incarnate, sacramental, and material dimension of Christianity. He says that "real love is not the love you see in a soap opera, a story that makes your heart beat a little faster but nothing more. Yes, the distant God of agnostics lacks concreteness" (Morning Meditation in Santa Marta of May 7, 2015).

We can talk a great deal about the handicapped and about the poorest and the neediest, but what they especially need from us are palpable signs, especially overcoming the fear they inspire in us. When we see a brother who is physically or mentally defective, what should we do? We should notice how Pope Francis always makes physical contact with people who approach him and are ill or suffering. He pampers them and devotes the better part of his audiences to them. As the head of the Church, and therefore a public personage who is closely observed every day by hundreds of thousands of people, he wants to show something very important: through physical acts, he makes visible the fundamental principle of the sacramental theology of the Incarnation. A credible affirmation that a person has dignity requires a palpable and visible love, expressed in concrete gestures. If we are to be sincere in our intention to live, not for ourselves, but for others, we must see the humble and often hidden acts of service by those who devote themselves to caring for the very young, the sick, the children, the elderly, as having an importance equal to that of the impressive scientific advances made by a university professor or the achievements of an entrepreneur who provides a decent job to many families. All of them are visible signs of the hope of Christ.

Let us also focus on the Christian vision of the family. Here, too, Christianity acts through the flesh, through a concrete way of communing and loving. All of these relationships are played out and decided, not in the intimate secrecy of a subjective consciousness, but in the visibility of a word given forever, of visible relationships with social consequences, of a concrete way of belonging to and building the Church. It is in these visible, concrete signs of the flesh that Christian love is manifested.

What you have told us about the importance of the body in Christianity implies as well a consideration that is distinct from the material, based on the Incarnation. Here, too, we said, a sphere for hope opens up. Can this shed light on the positive sciences, which have been considered since the beginning of modern times to be methodologically atheist, because they had to perform their experiments and calculations "as though God didn't exist"?

For centuries now, what the natural sciences or history have produced has been used to try to establish an agnostic attitude in the people of our comfort-centered societies. It would be gravely naïve of us not to recognize it. We sometimes overlook the army of Christian historians, scientists, and philosophers who have a scientific standing similar to or many times higher than that of others who boast about their rejection of Christianity. A great many scholarly Christians help us correct some assertions that are presented as being scientifically sound.

I think it is time to open up a truly unabashed dialogue—to challenge, humbly but decisively, the superiority complex of atheist thought and to discard our inferiority complex. We have every reason to confront purely psychological explanations of our faith or beliefs. We have good reasons to combine our faith in God with scientific and technological progress that, in itself, is an expression of our possibility of being coparticipants, with our intelligence and will, in the act of the creation.

Faith in God has never been and can never be an obstacle to scientific knowledge of the world. On the contrary, it is the opposite: it is precisely the surprised gaze of the believer, always searching for a unified vision of reality, that has the greatest capacity for finding the deep order with which God has imprinted his creation. The believer has always been alert to reality, aware that it always surpasses our understanding. The same faith in the resurrection of the flesh opens new horizons to our comprehension of the material world and also imparts new hope to science, because in its absence science would be locked up in repetitive schemes that overlook the surprising richness of the real.

Can this presumption to read reality "as if God didn't exist" also be seen in how our social coexistence is structured?

Yes, laicism, understood as an aggressive reaction to the phenomenon of religion, seeks the secularization of the state and often attributes, unfairly, a certain social violence to all religions, as generators of a supposed "intransigence" and "intolerance". We believers, however, live religion as revelation and God the Father and Creator's acceptance of all men, our brothers. We know that religion is absolutely contrary to violence and, of course, to murder in the name of the Creator.

In that connection, it must be clearly said that terrorism is not a religious phenomenon but a political ideology that clothes itself in pseudo-religious justification. I do not believe that the solution of the problem that has emerged in many of our societies that have great masses of immigrant populations who profess a different religion is to impose a radical nineteenth-century laicism, which only engenders more violence and more problems for future generations. The solution will come from entering a serious dialogue among all the believers of the various confessions and the rest of society, and doing so openly in accordance with applicable law.

I also think that modern democracy will be able to survive only if we continue to recognize that it is founded in human rights. Society cannot survive if individuals confine themselves to their selfish interests, seeking only their own pleasure and protecting themselves against their neighbor, whom they see as their enemy. More deeply, I believe that we have here a path out of the phenomenon of Islamist terrorism: we should not favor a separation of society as a whole from God, but should instead, on the contrary, harness the power of religion as a social relationship that reinforces living together, peace, and therefore progress for all.

The presumptuous authoritarian goal of privatizing religion, besides being founded on utterly questionable ideological hypotheses that have very problematic consequences, as we can see from a correct reading of the history of the twentieth century, is contrary to human rights and public liberties. Personal religion and ethics claim their social visibility because individuals are, in their complex totality, nothing other than interrelated social beings. Society, therefore, cannot be the sum of human atoms or lone individuals whose relations with each other are subject to the arbitrary approval of the powers that be: society is a living body made up of persons, not mechanical cogs who are manipulated in "social laboratories".

We can see from this that the hope Jesus brings us has been at work in history from the beginning. Saint Justin Martyr was one of the first to use the term "seeds of the Word" to refer to this hidden presence in the history of the harbingers of the Word. Now, though, we find that the expression "seeds of the Word" serves other ends. It has been said that certain kinds of union, such as "common-law couples" or mere cohabitation outside marriage, contain "seeds of the Word" and should be valued by Christians. What weight should be given to such explanations? Are "seeds of the Word" at work here, too?

To answer that question, let me lay out a theological reflection. Everything has been created in the *Logos*, in the Word. Creation is therefore not simply a collection of separate things, a pile of individual realities that subsequently enter into a relationship. On the contrary: all being is a representation of Being and God's goodness. Human knowledge and moral behavior are partakers of truth. Truth, on the other hand, is not merely an exterior object of our knowledge but is its own inner principle: whenever a scientist reaches a conclusion about a geological or biological phenomenon, a reflection of the truth that is God, the beginning and fullness of all, can ultimately always be read in this knowledge.

From this premise, I think we can better understand what the "seeds of the *Logos*" are. For the Fathers of the

Church, the Word, Jesus, had sown seeds of goodness in the world even before his Incarnation. They were advances on what he would manifest when he became incarnate. As seeds, they contained their own dynamism and movement that led the way toward him. These seeds were detectable in the behavior of many pagans, who did good deeds without knowing the true God. A good example was Socrates, who is considered a martyr or witness to God's truth to the point of death. Let us therefore not think of the seeds of the Word as something abstract or strange: when a mother who is not a Christian truly loves her child, she loves him with the love of God that is present in that relationship, although she does not know how to explain or articulate the fact that it involves the love of God. These are the "seeds of the *Logos*" that are at work in human relationships.

This thought made possible the rejection of that other, radically mistaken, vision that saw all the behavior of the pagans as simple vices. It is true that original sin, with all its consequences, exists. Original sin and personal sins result in the loss of our relationship with God, or gravely damage it. But that sin does not nullify human nature: that nature came from the hands of the Creator and is good (see Gen 1:31). No sin, however great it may be, can totally change the very dynamic of human nature, stamped on a body and in a soul that seeks to know and act. For example, a pagan who does not know Jesus Christ and solves a difficult mathematical equation or some obscure problem of physics does a good thing; his work is not contaminated by the fact that he is a pagan. On the contrary, his good professional work reflects the goodness of knowledge and intellect as they have been created by God. When a pagan builds a hospital, for example, even though he does not know that he is doing something good in the name of Jesus Christ, he still is serving Jesus Christ in the person of the sick. Without knowing it, he is doing something that is good and true in the eyes of God.

This principle does not legitimize immoral relationships, however, because the seeds of the Word do not abide in sinful situations such as cohabitation without marriage and other types of sexual unions. In these situations, despite the fact that it might seem otherwise, there can be no authentic dynamic of love but, rather, only a serious obstacle to the ability to grow in humanity. Another example, which today is stimulating a full debate: this principle could not be applied, either, to the situation of those who are divorced and remarried. The new marriage is again a serious obstacle, considering the emotional instability that it provokes in the subject, instability that is born anew in his affections and in any children there may be. I am aware that the problem of divorce is not an easy one to solve, nor do I believe that it is a question of casuistry, but it should not be posed as a matter of merely emotional issues, but considered, rather, with due seriousness and as a call for personal exigency.

The seeds God has sown certainly abide in the hearts of all persons, because all have a desire for true and full love. It will be the mission of the Church, Mother and teacher, to put that desire into relief, to validate it, and to make it grow: if necessary, even to denounce the structures, situations, and decisions that work against the truth of that love and impede the full, harmonious growth of the person.

Let us turn to Christ, this time particularly to Christ as the height of creation. From what you said before, faith in Jesus also gives us hope for temporal realities, throughout creation and human society. Can we hope that Christ reveals to us the meaning of things as a gift from the Father?

A Christian sees a very important relationship between the ultimate aim of everything, which is God, and the realities that lead us to the ultimate aim. According to what we read in Genesis, all of creation was good when it was made (see Gen 1:31). This goodness is reflected in all things by giving them a meaning in themselves, but also in the relationships that men establish with each other, with creation, and with God. All of creation chants the glory of God through the mouth of men (see Ps 8).

There are no great abstract thoughts in either the Old Testament or the New, such as those that, in contrast, can be found in Western philosophy. Scripture recounts the encounters of God and man in concrete realities: the planting, the rain, the harvest, the feast, children, work, sickness, and so on. It is in them that the covenant with God is shaped. Let us remember that the first promise God made to Israel was that they would occupy the Promised Land: "a land flowing with milk and honey" (Ex 33:3). Again, a reference to the concrete reality of basic foods. In an especially positive way, we see, too, that the Bible esteems manual labor and insists that the way to salvation lies through temporal and concrete things.

All of this is a radical break from Platonism, however much Nietzsche may say to the contrary in his first work, *The Birth of Tragedy*. According to this "master of suspicion", Christianity is nothing more than a popular Platonism for the simple folk, an escape from the world because their life is "weak, tired, doomed". The earthly has no more than passing value, like a step that helps us rise to what has true value, like a simple tool that can be discarded once it has served its purpose.

An in-depth study of the Old Testament reveals, however, how absolutely concrete everything in it is: God is petitioned to reveal his salvation, not in the hereafter, but in the everyday here and now. The Psalms, for example, reflect all the situations that are possible in life: instead of speaking directly of eternal life or the vision of salvation, instead of focusing on great ideas or general principles, we hear about the everyday, the nearby, the carnal: the peace that follows the battle, rain and the fruits of the earth, the fear of death, the tender love of a wife, or the desire to reach a happy old age. In them, the richness of life reveals itself in all its variety and color. The same thing happens in the books of wisdom, which contain some practical advice that is nothing more than good sense matured in simple day-to-day experience.

Jesus Christ is the high point of this concrete dynamic. His whole life is an expression of the carnal embodiment of the mystery: born of a woman, with only animals for company in the manger of shepherds who come in curiosity with their flocks; taken to Egypt as a newborn, fleeing from the political violence of the moment. All of these are concrete, possible, real situations. Even the very teaching of Jesus about the Kingdom of God is constructed in the same way: he takes examples from agricultural chores, from social life, or from the administration of justice in his day, as when he talks about the unrighteous judge [see Lk 18:2–8]. Rather than limiting himself to saying "God is just", Jesus explains divine justice through comparisons that are easily assimilable by everyone. Rather than devising a theory about love for one's neighbor, Jesus expounds it with parables that, in their simplicity, initiate the listener into the complexity of the mystery. Consider the Last Judgment, as it is described in Matthew 25: instead of conceptualizing there about good or evil, Jesus lists man's basic necessities, such as daily food, clothing, health, and company, inviting his listeners in concrete terms to love their neighbor.

Jesus' death on the Cross is the high point of realism in his message. He did not make a great speech beforehand; he did not gather all the political authorities to explain to them the meaning of his mission; he just died on a cross like a despicable condemned man shunned by everyone. "They shall look upon him whom they have pierced" (Jn 19:37). Instead of attaining an apotheosis, with his *mors turpissima crucis* (Cicero, *In verrem* 64, 65), he identified himself with the reality of suffering. From that Cross, Christ wanted to reveal the meaning of all temporal reality, introducing it into his mystery. Loving to the extreme of giving his life for us on the Cross, when we were not deserving of it, he proclaimed that all creation also has hope. In this way, he said that all that is good in the world is, indeed, a seed planted by God, called to maturity in his Kingdom under the constant and patient action of the Spirit. The Cross, in its monstrousness, reminds us that everything also has to undergo death, that maturity comes with suffering, that death does not destroy life but purifies it, saving and multiplying the good. I am moved when I recall the homily at the beginning of Pope Benedict XVI's pontificate, given in Saint Peter's Square on April 24, 2005, when he told us not to be afraid of Christ, because "he takes nothing away, and he gives you everything. When we give ourselves to him, we receive a hundredfold in return." For man, there is in Christ not a no but a great yes to all our hopes.

How far this concept is from the mere optimism fostered by a belief in the possibilities of man alone, alone in his understanding and striving! We know that if man's labors can bear fruit, it is because he opens himself up to someone greater who is working in him. Thus the ultimate hope of humanity, as Jesus taught us, is in God alone. To affirm this is not to imply denial of our natural and habitual trust in man or of the fraternal spirit but, instead, to highlight very accurately and realistically that our trust is born of our hope in God, our only Savior. The other realities are mere mediations of that unique salvation, and only Jesus offers us a well-founded hope.

Can you give us a further explanation of the relationship between the hopes we place in men and the great hope we place in God? We have lately learned of scandals involving priests that also show the difficulty of placing our ultimate hope in men.

Harmonious growth of the whole person absolutely requires placing trust in a parent, in older brothers, in teachers, in the priest, in persons who exercise authority. All of them not only guarantee that you will receive everything you need at this particular point in your life in which you are particularly fragile, they also are mediators of faith and trust in God. Your elders teach you to pray, to address God, to recognize your own personal vocation, and thereby to give your life full meaning. These individuals, when they are what they should be, are a blessing to you. They are your guides throughout your life, and when you have come to know them well, you never lose your gratitude and trust in them: in fact, you want to imitate them in the future.

But what if this person commits an offense that is public and notorious or, to put it more dramatically, becomes heretical or schismatic? What if he commits a crime? What happens then? What should we do? In this conflictive situation, we have to say, "Yes, this person has helped me deepen my faith, but I do not believe in him, I believe in God. He may have helped me accept faith or find my vocation, but it is Christ who has called me." What was a tragedy can be transformed into an occasion even of personal growth, for it helps you recognize that your ultimate trust must be placed only in God.

I think that another of today's great challenges is represented by the suffering of those who have experienced the betrayal of the trust they have placed in another person. They have placed their hope in him, they have trusted him completely, and they have been betrayed. I am not saying we have to avoid trusting in everything and everyone, that we have a reason to be sarcastic, skeptical, or bitterly ironic, that human nature is irremediably corrupted. I only mean that man is and always will be a weak creature and that we therefore cannot seek our support only in another person. Even the most loyal of men finally dies and leaves us on our own. Just for that reason, even when we are in the presence of an upright person who deserves our unconditional trust, we should consider the need not to make him the be-all and the end-all.

Let us recall the case of Jesus. In his Passion, when he was being threatened with death, all his disciples fled. They were not bad men, but they were beset by fear and doubt. Only God is always with us, until death, even though everyone else may have abandoned us. In situations of extreme despair, when there is no apparent solution, we can find consolation in God.

Certainly, the Church is the concrete and accessible presence of Jesus in the world. That is why the scandals committed by his ministers are particularly painful: in the responsibility I have to the Holy Father in the Disciplinary Section of the Congregation for the Doctrine of the Faith, which deals with certain offenses that are reserved for its consideration, among them the most serious ones (*delicta graviora*) committed by the clergy, I know whereof I speak. I can testify to the suffering and sadness caused by dealing daily with this terrible reality of the Church, both among my colleagues in the Dicastery and especially in the Holy Father, who ultimately reviews the most serious cases.

Throughout history, the Church has seen again and again that the priestly ministry is always tied to this radical frailty. I still remember the commotion caused by the words of then Cardinal Ratzinger in the ninth station of the Via Crucis of 2005 in the Coliseum: "How much uncleanness there is in the Church and among those who, in their priesthood, should devote themselves completely to it!"

But these very grave lapses and sins of banality, pride, lust, and so on, have not prevented the Church from continuing to spread the gospel with vigor, because all her strength comes from Christ. It is Christ who has assured the sanctity of the Church, and he has done it concretely and in the greatest abundance in the innumerable fruits of charity, wisdom, and forgiveness.

Hope in Christ, man's Redeemer, leads us now to the subject of the history and life of Jesus. One objection can be raised to the hope that Jesus brings us: Jesus of Nazareth lived and died two thousand years ago now; is it reasonable to be still awaiting something from him? On what basis can we reasonably count on and hope for something from a person who lived so long ago, who did not leave us any text written in his own hand, whose life and work have come down to us through so many mediations?

Historical documents do not enable a dead person to make himself truly present but only convey memories or interpretations of his acts. Those proofs of what happened in the past can stimulate our fantasies and imagination or sharpen our intellect in discussing the arguments involved. But the people who appear in them are not truly present: it is only possible to overcome the intervening spatio-temporal distance if those people are still alive.

What you are positing in your question only happens with the Risen One. The Lord is not present through a book or a recording of his voice, through his meditations or theories. It is recognized that he is alive in the Church through his acts, through the fact that he continues to act in baptism and in making himself present with his divinity and humanity in the Eucharist.

Saint Thomas Aquinas says the reason Christ left us nothing written in his own hand was that he preferred another form of transmission: through forming disciples. It was to them that he delivered his living presence in the sacraments, for transmission with the witness of their own lives. Thus, because Christ is present in real and sacramental form in the Church, we can understand and accept that his Word is what their apostolic witness reflects in the Gospels and Epistles. Christ himself is present in and guides these readings. The same Christ who gives us life, who gives us Communion, brings himself to life for us in this way. This same Christ is also present in prayer. The spatial and temporal distance is bridged only when he himself makes himself present.

The great figures of history, Caesar, Augustus, Alexander, can be almost visibly present, for example in a film. But we all know that the actor is not the actual Alexander the Great: he is a construct of our imagination that we portray theatrically. That figure enters into our imagination.

In Christ, reality radically surpasses all these expectations. The same Word that is God is present in us when we read Holy Scripture, not as mere fantasy or autosuggestion, but in the form of him who truly speaks with me. The mediation of Holy Scripture and the living subject of this Word, who is Christ Jesus, are one. We therefore come into contact with the living Word of Jesus, who speaks to me through the word of men.

Easter and faith in the Resurrection of Jesus played a singular role in this witness.

That is right. The Resurrection is not something that can be verified empirically: faith is always required. Already in Jesus' time, when he walked the roads of Galilee and Judea in the flesh, as a mortal, his contemporaries could not prove empirically that the man who was speaking to them was the Son of God because they had not seen the act of Incarnation. There were many others who said: "I am the Messiah." There were also several who made signs. The disciples put their faith, however, in Jesus. It was especially in the apparitions of the Risen One that they were convinced that Jesus, objectively, was speaking to them. And they went from being a group of frightened men, who in sorrow and even a certain shame had been prepared to return to their previous occupations, to going forth proclaiming to all, at risk to their lives, that Jesus, he who had been crucified, was alive. This singular event, transmitted in the early years by oral tradition among those post-Paschal communities, was recorded in writing by the evangelists to preserve it in its entirety for future generations. The witness of this fact continues to manifest itself today in our communities of faith: we all can participate in it, observe its reflection in our lives, and confirm it with our mission.

In this our brief excursion through the origins of the Gospels and their transmission to us, what manifests itself is the strength of faith yet also its fragility, because it requires the assent of mortal man. A man of faith should always pray: "I believe; help my unbelief!" (Mk 9:24). We can never in our human lifetime overcome this fragility and the constant effort that faith requires. We will always have to renew it and ask for help in doing so, relying as a Church on our brothers.

Does this mean that empirical proofs can never confirm our faith, that we therefore have to seek some other form of "credibility"?

We normally say that critical study of historical documentation or repetition of experiments in a laboratory offers us scientific assurance and certainty. But the elements of empirical proof do not give us the certainty we need to accept this concrete fact of faith called "resurrection". We know it is impossible to revive a cadaver by ourselves. We do, nevertheless, have proven testimony to the Resurrection: Christ appeared to his disciples, and they had an inner certainty, based on revelation, that they had not fallen prey to autosuggestion. As we just said, they even gave their lives for that. Through faith founded on the apostles' testimony, we who come after Jesus' disciples believe in what they saw and touched in the presence of the Word of life.

In any case, faith always puts our freedom into play. Faith is an act that is particular to human freedom, a voluntary encounter with God, who is absolute truth. In my freedom, I am the one who has to say yes to the personal encounter with the person of Christ. We believers know, on the other hand, that we receive from the Holy Spirit the gift of welcoming the witness we receive and giving it our free assent of faith.

Actually, this form of knowledge particular to faith has already begun in our interpersonal encounters. I cannot prove a man's happiness in the same way that I learn how a computer works. I turn on the computer, and if it works well, it responds immediately when I press a button. But I cannot ascertain whether a man is happy just by pressing a button. There is a dimension of truth there that substantially, and not just gradually, transcends material things and empirical facts. Trust can be another example of things that transcend the merely empirical: let us imagine a person whom I have known for many years, with whom I have an extremely close friendship, and who, I am convinced, loves and esteems me. If this person tells me, "I need fifty euros", I will give them to him if I have them and can afford to. I do not even ask him what he needs them for. I am not empirically certain of the usefulness of what he will do with them. For that reason a scientific experiment makes no sense in close relationships: How can it be verified in a laboratory?

If the Creator reveals himself in his own Son in order to give his life for us, if this Creator, the Father, tells me and reveals to me that his Son is my Savior and I can place my absolute trust in him, I will tend to believe and rely on this word. Because only the Creator can also be the Savior. It is not that we have a physical certainty, but something much more important: we have an existential certainty, which opens us up to all existence.

Based on that certainty, the disciples began to preach. What they preached lit a new worldwide fire of love for Jesus that gave corporeality to his surprising words throughout history. These words, which can seem to be no more than a beautiful unattainable ideal, have taken flesh generation after generation. This is the other element of credibility for our faith. The hope that Jesus brings us now passes through the Church. The mission of the Church is to transmit this hope.

II

WHAT CAN WE HOPE FOR
FROM THE CHURCH?

*The last question we posed opens a new part of our interview.
Jesus founded the Church, through which his living Word is
transmitted; but what can we hope for from the Church? Light
and companionship? Of what kind?*

As I said before, faith in Jesus Christ is not just a desire, an
illusion, an autosuggestion, a private and subjective matter
that affects only me. For the Church is the communion of
all who believe in Jesus: she is therefore a community
based on faith, but she also has an institutional dimension,
acting in the name of Jesus and representing him as the
Good Shepherd and Master. In doing so, she performs a
teaching, sanctifying, and governing function, embracing
in these three categories the whole of Jesus' mission of
salvation. In that definition lies all that we can and should
hope for from the Church.

We must be careful, however, not to confuse Christ's
true Church with the image of her that is so often distorted
in its presentation by the media or by those who are not
a part of her and speak of her as just another institution.
Even less should we confuse her with the caricature by
which she is depicted by those who want only to criti-
cize her.

The Church is a divine reality, not a purely sociological, empirical fact that can be verified through her exterior functions. These are certainly signs of Jesus' action through the Church. But the Church, as such, is a work and consequence of salvation and is shaped by the Incarnation. God made himself man, and men who gather around his Son make God visible in this world.

There are those who say that Jesus realized his plan of salvation and then, shortly before he departed, founded an organization to administer and transmit a supernatural faith. There is a well-known statement by the modernist theologian A. Loisy (*L'Église et l'Évangile*) that has been repeated as a slogan ad nauseam: "Jesus preached the Kingdom of God, but what we got was the Church." This gloss is totally insufficient, because the Church is a supernatural reality, not just a natural one. If salvation is a divine work, so is the medium of its transmission, even if it acts and evolves in this world. That is the origin of the analogy between Christ, as God and true man, and the Church as divine grace humanly transmitted.

The two great, opposing Christological heresies are monophysitism, which holds that Christ exists only in his divine nature, and Nestorianism, which affirms the existence in Christ of two perfect natures, each with its own personal realization. Both have had ecclesiological repercussions. On the one hand, there is ecclesiological naturalism, which sees the human realization as something perfect and realized in itself; and on the other, there is the divinization of the Church, in which she is seen as exclusively divine.

In this regard, traditional Protestant theology establishes a great distance, even a yawning divide, between "Christ the Head" and "the Church the Body of Christ". For my part, I think this image of a head and a body, from Saint

Paul, contains in it not only the difference between Christ and the Church but also what unites them: as Saint Augustine of Hippo magisterially expressed it: *unus Christus, caput et corpus*—that is, "Christ is one, the Head and the Body."

What other one-sided visions of the Church could be cited?

The mystery of the Church is multi-dimensional. No theological system should impose itself unilaterally when it comes to trying to clarify this mystery. I can develop an ecclesiology that highlights the canonical aspects, for example, which would emphasize the element of canon law. This explanation, although meaningful, would run the risk of being one-sided if it failed to integrate the life of faith and the body of expressions of the mystery that is the Church.

The Enlightenment, for example, saw the emergence of a convenient conception of the Church, based on pragmatism and liberalism, that considered that she existed only to give simple folk a moral education. There then followed a romantic vision, which conceived of the Church as a mere ideal, disregarding the sinners who were her members. Then came a political vision, linking her to the fight for social justice in the world. And so on up to the present. The Church's mission is something else, however: she brings people to Christ, preaching the gospel to them and celebrating and realizing for them the saving acts of Christ in the Word, in the sacraments, and in the pastors' accompaniment of the faithful.

The Eucharist, in fact, is celebrated in the Church. But at the same time, we can say that "the Church was born of the Eucharist."

The theologian Henri de Lubac has expressed this idea in masterly fashion. Can you clarify for us the relationship between the Church and the Eucharist?

The Church exists as such, in her structure and her mission, once and for all. She celebrates the Eucharist by the commandment of Christ, and the faithful are thereby comforted and nourished with Holy Communion. There is therefore a permanent internal identification of the Church with the Eucharist, though they are not two entities of the same order. The Church thus celebrates the sacraments for the faithful and is in that way the instrument by which grace is conveyed, but at the same time she is in herself a sign of grace, because she serves the nourishment that the faithful receive in the Eucharist, christifying them. The Eucharist makes the Church and is made in the Church.

The texts of the New Testament attest to the intimate union of the two. In the First Letter to the Corinthians, Saint Paul speaks of the institution of the Eucharist (1 Cor 11) with a clear reference to the simile with the body, on which he then proceeds to elaborate (1 Cor 12). Also, a Eucharistic reference in his Letter to the Romans precedes the instructions on fraternal relations and the mutual love that develops around the simile with the body: to offer a living sacrifice, a pleasing offering (Rom 12). Saint Paul thus saw the indissoluble relationship between the two realities: the one Body of the Church and the Eucharistic offering of Christ through his Church and in his Church.

Who is the Church to impose a series of requirements for those who come to receive Communion? Saint Augustine says that when a communicant in the Eucharist answers "Amen", it is because he wants to become the Body of Christ: *"When you hear 'The Body of Christ', you reply 'Amen.' Be a member of Christ's Body, then, so that your 'Amen' may ring true!"* (*Sermon 272:1*). Receiving Communion, therefore, implies saying yes to the exigency of life in the Body of Christ, which is the Church. Might this not be an excessive claim? Would it not be more logical to say that our amen is the expression of a desire, of an "I wish" but "still cannot", and therefore I entrust myself to Christ's mercy? The question touches on a decisive point, which is the relationship that exists between grace and conversion, between the sacrament and the change in one's life. From the beginning, the Church required conversion in the catechumen, demanding a life change before baptism. Would it not be more consistent to baptize first and then require the life change?

Pope Francis says in his *Evangelii gaudium* (47) that the Eucharist "is not a prize for the perfect but a powerful medicine and nourishment for the weak". This statement deserves to be analyzed deeply so as not to mistake its meaning.

In the first place, it should be pointed out that this affirmation expresses the primacy of grace: conversion is not an autonomous act of man; rather, it is in itself an act of grace. But that cannot justify the conclusion that conversion is an external reply of thanks for what God has done in me, though he has done it alone, without me. Nor can I conclude that anyone can come to receive the Eucharist even though he is not in grace and does not have the required state of mind, just because it is nourishment for the weak.

We should ask, first and foremost, what is conversion? It is a free act of man and, at the same time, an act motivated by the grace of God that always precedes the acts of men. It is therefore an integral act, incomprehensible if God's act is separate from that of man. Theology has succeeded in going beyond the great question that was posed by the rigid scheme that separated God's act from the human response: instead of thinking of them as taking place at separate times, their collaboration should be understood as a joint effort, a divine act that penetrates and transforms human existence from within, to the point where it results in a true divinization. Looking at it that way, we understand that conversion is not a prize but is, rather, first an act of grace to which man responds freely.

In the sacrament of penance, for example, one can see very clearly the need for a free response on the part of the penitent, expressed in his heartfelt contrition, his intention to change his ways, the confession of his sins, his expiation. Catholic theology therefore denies that God does it all and man is only a recipient of the divine graces. Conversion is both the new life that is given us through grace and, at the same time, a task that is offered us as a condition of continuing grace.

In reality, the significance of conversion can only be understood in the logic of love, because he who loves desires the response of the beloved and, loving him, elicits it. Did Saint Paul not say that "while we were [still] enemies", God showed "his love for us" (Rom 5:10, 8)? It is precisely his love that has transformed us from enemies into friends.

Does Eucharistic Communion, then, come with "preconditions"?

There are only two sacraments that establish the state of grace: baptism and the sacrament of reconciliation. When one has lost sanctifying grace, he needs the sacrament of reconciliation to recover it, not because he himself deserves it, but as a gift, a gift that God offers him in sacramental form. Certainly access to Eucharistic Communion presupposes a life of grace, presupposes communion in the Body of the Church, and also presupposes a life ordered in conformity with the Body of the Church so as to be able to say the "Amen" to which you referred before. Saint Paul insists that whoever eats the bread or drinks the cup of the Lord in an unworthy manner will be guilty of profaning the Body and Blood of the Lord (1 Cor 11:27).

Saint Augustine says that "God who created you without you will not save you without you" (Sermon 169). God asks for my collaboration. A collaboration that is also his gift but that entails my acceptance of it. If things were otherwise, we could succumb to the temptation of thinking of the Christian life as being akin to mere mechanics. Forgiveness, for example, would be something automatic, almost mandatory, rather than a request that also depends on me, because I am the one who has to make it. So I would go to Communion without being in the required state of grace and without passing through the sacrament of reconciliation. I would even take it for granted, with no evidence for it based on the Word of God, that he grants me privately the forgiveness of my sins for this same Communion. This is a false concept of God; this is tempting him. It also involves a false concept of man, by undervaluing what God can enkindle in him.

I would like to consider now another aspect: Can we hope for something from the Church as an institution? Lumen gentium *(no. 8) says that the Church is holy and at the same time in need of purification, embracing sinners in her bosom as she does. What can we expect from the hierarchy, especially in the context of the scandals that continually stain it?*

Jesus said that there will always be scandals in the Church but later added: "Woe to him by whom they come." We know that in the fallen state of human nature, there is an inclination toward sin and that the power of sin is at work in every man. It is not only that there are saints and sinners: we recognize concupiscence, moral frailty, in every man.

The Church is holy in her link with Jesus Christ, in her sacramental institutions, in acts of grace and proclamation of the Word of God, but her members are men and can fall into sin. I am not talking here only about trivial everyday sins, the failings and weaknesses that we all experience, but also about serious sins.

Anyone who understands this will be able to stay out of the game of the Church's enemies, who are always looking for new ways to discredit her. In an accusation that is unquestionably pharisaic, her enemies say: "You want to teach us God's commandments, which we reject, and you yourselves are not capable of obeying the commandments you want to impose on us." Some media or the sensationalist press that benefit from these scandals, whether they are true or not, also use these arguments. But are they valid arguments? Is it not a case of wanting to confuse in this way the "treasure of the gospel" with the "earthen vessels" that carry and transmit it?

The true faithful certainly suffer when a representative of the Church falls into a sin that produces a serious public scandal. But we must not allow this reality to sow doubt or despair in us. History, as ever, is also life's teacher here. Certain periods in the history of the Church have been truly appalling, as when there were popes or bishops who did not concern themselves in the least with faith or the moral life. There was a truly dark time in the Church of the High Middle Ages, for example, among other very difficult periods. The temptation in these difficult periods was also to seek refuge in an ideal Church, an invisible Church. But attaining the goal of an ideal, totally pure Church in history failed in the end because the prophets of that goal, those who attempted to promote it, could not change the human condition under the influence of sin.

In saying that, I do not intend at all to excuse the pastors of the Church. We must shun the double life and the scandal that it entails; we must shun failing to take our commitments seriously; we must shun, too, underhanded dealings with the world. But the Christian faithful should know that faith and the relationship with God cannot be conditioned on priests being absolutely free from sin. That is impossible. On the other hand, we priests know from experience that we must take the most meticulous care of our spiritual life: assiduous confession, moments of intimacy with the Lord in silent adoration, praying the breviary for the whole Church, entrusting ourselves to the maternal care of Mary, the hard work of spiritual exercises every year, and above all the devout celebration of Christ's sacrifice in daily Mass. We, too, are enveloped in misery, and therefore we need a firm piety and the continual forgiveness of God if we want to renew our Christian life and, specifically, the commitment we undertook one day to serve the Church for life, out of love for Christ.

It is not right, for example, that the media, especially at times that are particularly relevant to our life of faith such as the days before Easter, should magnify the woes of priests and suppress all mention of the exemplary and faithful lives led by the great majority of the clergy. So many priests are true "shepherds living with the 'odor of the sheep'" (Pope Francis' homily of Holy Thursday, March 28, 2013), always at the side of the poor, the sick, the young, the families. So many priests offer their lives and dedicate themselves, with all their hopes and all their strength, with the help of grace, to the expansion of the Kingdom of God and the mission of the Church. A more realistic, impartial vision, free of any spurious agenda, entails the painful acceptance of human frailty, as Saint Paul accepted it in the Second Letter to the Corinthians when he talked about the joys and exigencies of the apostolic ministry.

The Church is holy because of her relationship with God, and at the same time she is sinful because she is made up of sinful men. The dogmatic constitution *Lumen gentium* tells us in paragraph 8: "While Christ, holy, innocent, and undefiled [Heb 7:26], knew nothing of sin [2 Cor 5:21], but came to expiate only the sins of the people [Heb 2:17], the Church, embracing in its bosom sinners, at the same time holy and always in need of being purified, always follows the way of penance and renewal."

And when the Church does beg forgiveness? From whom? For what?

The Church begs forgiveness from God in the first instance because only God can forgive sins. But also from those who feel themselves wounded by the acts of her members. The Church, in fact, has on some public occasions begged forgiveness in the person of the pope, Vicar of Christ on earth: in that connection, we all recall that in the Jubilee Year of 2000, Saint John Paul II made a heartfelt plea for forgiveness by confessing the sins of the men of the Church and inviting Christians "to acknowledge, before God and before those offended by their actions, the faults which they have committed".

Afterward, the International Theological Commission published the text "Memory and Reconciliation: The Church and the Faults of the Past" to explain the exact meaning of this request for forgiveness. Several questions were posed there: Why should the request be made? Who should make it? What is the goal, and how, in the right combination of historical and theological judgment, should that be determined? To whom will it be addressed? What are its moral implications? What are the possible effects on the life of the Church and on society?

Reaching a correct historical judgment on the past is not always simple, and in fact it is frequently blocked by prevailing prejudices. At the same time, it must be made clear that this *confession of sin* should be framed within the confession of God's glory. The Church, confessing her sin, must first and foremost confess the glorious acts of God.

In addition, the request for forgiveness must be understood within the framework of the many persecutions suffered by Christians throughout history. The history of the Church is not a shameful history that has to be covered with a plea for pardon. On the contrary, it is a history of grace marked by the testimony of a great many saints, many of them martyrs. A fact like the evangelization of the Americas can be seen as an occasion to highlight mistakes and sins, of which there were some, but above all to give thanks that that admirable act of faith and civilization, in which some Europeans, mainly Spaniards of the sixteenth century, gave that "new world", generously and even heroically, the best of what they had—that is, their faith. What would Mexico be without its devotion to the Virgin of Guadalupe? What would the Americas be without the renowned cultural work done in the universities that emerged under the sponsorship of the Church? Catholicism will always be indebted to the missionary and evangelizing impetus of Spain.

From that perspective, the Church's request for forgiveness has an exemplary and prophetic value, as much for other religions as for governments and other social institutions. It is striking that there has almost never been a comparable plea for forgiveness from other sectors of society. I am talking, for example, about today's ultraliberals, who have stepped into the shoes of those who in the nineteenth century so diligently suppressed the civil liberties of the Church; or about the Communists and radical politicians who have imposed sectarian laws like the Mexican constitution of 1917 or the "Calles Law" of 1926, which gave rise to the terrible Cristero War in that country, with its thousands of deaths; or also about politicians of the extreme right, the heirs of National Socialism or Fascism; or, finally, about those who have tried through the media to eliminate the Christian religion from the public square, who ostensibly in the name of freedom of expression have incited, tolerated, or applauded vile attacks against the Church or those who have stolen properties from the Church or benefited from them as heirs, and about so many others, whom we won't continue to list, who have never asked for forgiveness.

Again, what I am saying is not an attempt to excuse or exonerate ourselves. As Saint John Paul II pointed out, this purification of memory is "an act of courage and humility in recognizing the wrongs done by those who have borne or bear the name of Christian", and it is based on the conviction that "because of the bond which unites us to one another in the Mystical Body, all of us, though not personally responsible and without encroaching on the judgment of God, who alone knows every heart, bear the burden of the errors and faults of those who have gone before us."

What can we hope for from the pope? What does Christ expect from him? This question might be understood in the context of the Protestant accusation that has considered Catholics to be "papists". Are we Catholics "papists"? A contemporary theologian has defined "sacramentalism" as follows: "Sacramentalism is, in all its manifestations and forms, the identification *of the visible Church with the invisible, of the infallibility of the pope with the infallibility of Christ, of the acts of priests with Christ's acts, of the liturgy with the event that was Jesus Christ." Is this a real risk?*

It is true that a false papism can arise: it does so when the pope is the object of exaggerated admiration as a public figure, as a kind of world leader, as an eminent personage comparable to a famous actor or well-known politician. This is papism that would be appropriate for a worldly ecclesiology, which has been so criticized by Pope Francis.

There does exist, however, a form of respect and love for the pope that is very different from what I have just described. We love him because we see in him the successor to Peter, the permanent foundation of the unity of the Church with Christ and the unity of local Churches among themselves, in which we are confirmed by the faith that Jesus revealed and transmitted in the tradition of the Church.

Again, we must be on guard against attempts to construct two parallel Churches, one visible and the other invisible, one sinful and the other holy, one institutional and the other spiritual. That is not how it is. What is sometimes called the invisible Church, that is, the communion of the faithful in grace, cannot be understood without the visible Church, which is the expression of this intimate union in the sacraments and in its concrete manifestations in this world.

We must avoid, and when necessary overcome, all Christological and ecclesiological dualism. The Church with her sacramental institutions serves Christ, and Christ avails himself of his Church. Strictly speaking, her ministers never act in their own name: only God gives grace and supernatural life. God does it through the sacramental authority of the ministers, who function, not as a machine, but as living instruments. As shepherds and servants of Christ, they are required to conform to special norms in their celebration, which differentiates them from the hirelings of the parable (Jn 10:1–21). Distinguishing but not separating, we understand that there are no false alternatives but, rather, an intimate unity between Christ and the minister.

Specifically, it is true that a populist vision of the pope could arise, a devotion based on mere sentiments of sympathy or even, in the worst cases, for the sake of personal benefit. This last can arise, too, in any ecclesiastical ambit: a priest friend of mine told me that a newly ordained priest in his diocese, on the religious stamps commemorating his first Mass, had written "God is love (Paul VI)", almost as though an attribution of this formulation to the pope were more authoritative than an attribution to Saint John, its true source.

At the same time, we cannot regard the pope as though he were simply a companion or the highest functionary of the Church. The pope is a person with a spiritual mission, with a very singular and illustrious vocation, authorized by Christ to act in his name. The respect that his singular calling requires, to confirm us all in our faith, has a religious foundation and is the basis for our profound and devoted filial love for him.

Let us continue now with another subject having to do with the ecclesiastical hierarchy. What can we hope for from the bishops? A bishop might reduce himself to being the administrator of a diocese,

but then what should we hope for from him? Merely an adequate
pastoral administration and financial management?

Revelation establishes a very clear order among the various obligations of the bishop: appointed by the Holy Spirit
to represent Jesus Christ, he also preaches the gospel as a
servant of the Word and guides his flock as its shepherd, to
testify to and defend their store of faith and all the revealed
truths through which we are joined with God as the fount
of truth.

The bishop is the unifying principle of all the pastors
and faithful in his diocese and, at the same time, together
with the other bishops, represents apostolic authority and
the apostolic succession, *cum et sub Petro*. That is the great
mission of the bishop: "God's steward" (Tit 1:7).

We should make it clear that that stewardship does not
mainly consist in financial management of the diocese but,
rather, first and foremost, in the pastoral governance of
the house that is the Church of God. Being a good pastor,
devoted to the care of his faithful, is much more than simply keeping good accounts or being a good communicator
respected by the media. It is therefore understood that the
bishop, first and foremost, should be someone devoted to
serving the Lord and the local Church entrusted to his
care, in the manner of a faithful spouse, someone who
does not waver in his orthodoxy and who celebrates and
lives the faith of the Church in its entirety.

And what can we hope for from the bishops' conferences? What
is their significance? This naturally also involves the relations
between local Churches and the universal Church. How should
we think about them? The question is especially relevant today
given the hypothesis that it is in the bishops' conferences that

questions related to doctrine, or to discipline rooted in doctrine, are resolved.

The bishops' conference is not the local Church, because the political division into countries or regions is not an immediate theological or dogmatic principle. These groupings of local Churches according to political, linguistic, cultural, or social factors do not have any more authority than the sum of the authority of all the bishops who belong to them.

The episcopal conferences certainly have a reason for being by virtue of the fact that the spirit of collegiality requires a way to work together efficiently and collaborate responsibly. For example, when a common catechism is needed, when liturgical books need to be published in a particular language, when the right pedagogical materials in a particular region need to be prepared, or when a common spokesman before the civil organisms of the nation involved is needed.

The Church, however, is not a federation of episcopal conferences, presided over by a world president, nor is she an aggregation of communities. The Church is one, in the confession of the same faith in the same Lord and in the same baptism. The pope, for his part, is bishop of the local Church of Rome and the permanent principle of the unity of the faith, in the communion of the sacraments and in doctrine. Yes: the Church is one in the means of sanctification, and it is her natural role to unite all men in the same family of God, as we see in the episode of Pentecost, when the disciples understood each other even though they were speaking in all languages: by the action of the Holy Spirit, the division epitomized by the Tower of Babel was reversed, making the unity of the one Body of Christ recognizable.

Let us recall that "catholic" means universal. The Catholic Church is, therefore, what unites all men in Christ and not merely the church that joins them in joint action in this world. Those who see the Church solely in terms of power speak of the president, the executive committee, or the secretariat of the episcopal conference as if they were speaking of the members of a financial or industrial corporation. As a result, the episcopal conference would fall into a new form of centralization, only without any foundation in ecclesiology and with the purpose of substituting a "provincial centralism" for "Roman centralism". With the added problem that the former would cast doubt on the fact that the Church of Rome is the principle of the Church's unity.

The Second Vatican Council achieved a sensible balance among all the local Churches, one of which is the Church of Rome, and the universal Church, formed by the communion of all the Churches under the guidance of the bishop of Rome. I believe we need to deepen and preserve this balance. We have often heard complaints of the "Roman centralism" mentioned earlier, in protest against the bishop of Rome's way of guiding the universal Church. Yet objection is not always raised against the fact that this manner of speaking, using a seductive but mistaken and inappropriate category, is a falsification of the truth of the Church. If we were to return to what I call the balance of Vatican II, we could avoid repeating some ecclesiological errors of the past, like papism and priestism, on the one hand, or conciliarism and gallicanism, on the other.

There is a real danger today that these false antagonisms will again come to the fore, with the grave consequences they would have on what is more important for the present: I am talking about the new evangelization, which is impossible to carry out without the help of the Spirit and the cooperation of everyone everywhere. A centripetal movement that would fragment the Church into local autonomous communities offers no guarantee that the Church would be closer to the needs of a given culture or country. On the contrary: the apostolic strength of the Church would be impoverished because it would attack communion—that is, the intimate union of all men among themselves and with God.

We should therefore make a special effort not to allow ourselves to harbor the slightest sign of the anachronistic anti-Roman complex, which has its origin in the prejudices and resentments of the past. But we should also avoid any temptation to fragment the Church, conceiving of her as a federation of associations of like members in which everyone will fit: perhaps this conception of the Church would sell well and be met with applause from the media in the short term, but I am quite certain that such a reality could never receive the blessing of the Holy Spirit.

Let me take the occasion to ask another question that has emerged in the last few months, in the context of the Synod on the Family. There was discussion there of the "principle of synodality", that is, of a Church that is advancing and in dialogue: What can be said about that? Of what does this "principle of synodality" in the Church consist?

The recent thinking about the synodality of the Church, as it shares (*syn*) a road (*odos*) in moving through history toward the definitive coming of the Lord, is legitimate and necessary because, without touching on either the communion among the people of God or their origin and essence, it attempts to develop a better analysis of the inner principle of certain institutions that are important to the life of the Church and her mission, like the organs of participation (*CIC*, can. 212 §3).

Certainly, the recent Synod on the Family of 2015 wisely affirmed that all the faithful must participate more in the decision-making process of the Church, linking this thinking to the concept of synodality.

Notwithstanding what was reported by some of the media, the objective of this analysis has nothing to do with a presumed need to democratize the Church at all levels. Democracy is a way of organizing human society with the aim of achieving the participation of everyone in the group, in some form, in the election of those exercising power and the adoption of its laws. In its many variations, it is one of many ways that respect human dignity in governing human society.

In any case, the Church is not a human institution that structures itself but rather the people of God, whom God himself directs in the exercise of his absolute sovereignty: in her, all are invited to participate in her mission, although not all in the same way: "The Christian faithful are those who, inasmuch as they have been incorporated in Christ through baptism, have been constituted as the people of God; for this reason, since they have become sharers in Christ's priestly, prophetic and royal office in their own manner, they are called to exercise the mission which God has entrusted to the Church to fulfill in the world, in accord with the condition proper to each one" (*CIC*, can. 204 §1).

The profound equality of all the faithful as children of God and their functional diversity described in the canon quoted above are reflected in the decision-making processes of the Church. In that connection, the *supernaturalis sensus fidei* (*Lumen gentium*, no. 12)—the prophetic and common sense of faith that gives all the baptized, through the inspiration of the Spirit, a sound orientation—is often invoked to argue mistakenly for a democratization of faith on the basis of the need to give weight in the Church to the private and subjective opinion of each of the faithful. To put it in simple terms, I would say that the *sensus fidei* is a kind of antenna that, with the help of the Holy Spirit, enables me to understand the revelation of God in Jesus Christ. But it is never a parallel or independent instance of the Magisterium of the Church.

Pastors also participate in the *sensus fidei*, but only they have the charism of discernment. This is exercised, above all, in the college of bishops, in solemn form in the ecumenical council, and ordinarily through the bishops around the world in communion with the Apostolic See, for they are "the successors of the apostles" in the Magisterium and pastoral government (see *Lumen gentium*, no. 22). The synod of bishops, specifically, is a weak form of episcopal collegiality in action: the college of bishops is represented in it by only a limited number of its members, and its resolutions ordinarily are not binding ("unless the Roman Pontiff in certain cases has endowed the synod with deliberative power" [*CIC*, can. 343]).

A healthy debate about synodality in the Church should therefore avoid any form of dualism: on the one hand, all the faithful must commit themselves to the dissemination of the Word of God, but this will not be possible if the common priesthood is set against and confused with the ministerial priesthood (see *Lumen gentium*, no. 10). In any case, it is necessary that the pope by his *munus petrinum* and each bishop *cum Petro*, never *sine Petro*, expressing the *unio collegialis* that befits the affective collegiality through which he shares the solicitude for the common good of the whole Church in explicit exercises of jurisdiction (effective collegiality), advance as far as possible in those forms of collegiality that will optimize the ecclesial discernment that is characteristic of them, without committing errors such as administering the Church collegially or considering the pope as a simple representative of unity, a facilitator, an organizer, or a mere arbiter. When God distributes his charisms in the Church, he does not contradict himself: he is the same Spirit, whether he is working in some or in others.

And what can we hope for from priests? There is a story about a teacher in seminary who told his students: "The priest is first and foremost a preacher of the gospel; if you also live the gospel, so much the better." It would seem that, with this perspective, puritanism and moralism have been deemphasized in the evaluation of priests. So I would like to ask you, is there not a risk that the constant accusations of "phariseeism" against priests will end up making them shrink from preaching and the mission that is entrusted to them?

I think this comment illuminates an important point, but let me introduce a nuance. The general principle is that the priest preaches the gospel with his word and with his life: in fact, with his life he highlights the credibility of the gospel. Since credibility is one thing and fallibility is another, the gospel does not lose its credibility because a priest falls into sin.

In any case, we have to remember that the apostles did not preach their own word but, rather, the Word of God. Saint Paul explains in his First Letter to the Thessalonians that "our gospel came to you not only in word, but also in power and in the Holy Spirit and with full conviction" (1 Thess 1:5). And in the Acts of the Apostles we are told about Paul's reaction when they wanted to adore him as a god because he had cured a paralytic (Acts 14:8–9): he had to make it clear that he had not acted in his own name but in the name of God, which is what he was proclaiming to them.

We, too, preach the gospel and moral principles, but not because they are our principles. We are not the authors of doctrine or moral principles but, rather, just witnesses to them and, compliantly, we also follow them. We priests, therefore, ought to be the first to obey the Word of God: before preaching it, we ourselves should listen to it, study it carefully, pray it with devotion, live it without the least self-referentiality. We are sowers of seeds, with no pretension to being the ones who will reap the harvest. We are simple instruments of Christ crucified, with no pretension to being greater than our Master and, therefore, to being successful in human terms in our ministry.

We priests should be more careful with the ministry of the Word. By the grace of God, we treat the Body of Christ with great reverence and respect, but I often observe that we do not do the same with the Word: so many times do we prepare our sermons inadequately, confess that preaching is tiresome to us, or even hesitate to preach the full gospel for fear of the world's accusations! Let us not ignore, either, the fact that some of those who govern our societies are keenly interested in silencing Christian preaching, especially when it exposes their underhanded attempts to control social ideology. To do that, they do not hesitate to make fun of the doctrine of the Church and deprecate priests, if by doing so they can attain their goal. We cannot lower our guard: let us take care not to be intimidated, because the Lord has promised us his help, every day, until the end of the world (see Mt 28:20).

Bearing witness to the gospel, is this the best "pastoral method" of evangelizing?

After many years' pastoral experience of many kinds, I think perhaps it is time to deepen the concept of the "pastoral method". I for one tend to have little confidence in an insistence that the solution to the secularization of a diocese or a parish lies in the application of a new pastoral theory or that "now the liturgy should be reconfigured in this new way to be credible and participative." Behind these declarations, it is not hard to find a line of reasoning based on simply human postulates that, proposing laboratory pastoral recipes, is pursuing the ingenuous aspiration of solving all problems.

"We have to come up with a new road for the Church of the future", "the Church has to change", "the Church has to do this and that", "the Church is antiquated and out of step." Those who say such things are then generally incapable of framing intelligent proposals or coming up with sensible solutions, nor do they have the strength to bring them to fruition. They say to us: "the Church has to change her terminology", "today's Church has to abandon the old pastoral methods", "the Church has to ..." Unfortunately, such statements only feed other, similar slogans that, without leading to any real, positive change, elicit the perennial complaint and the most sterile discouragement.

The pastoral logic that is manifest in the gospel, however, which is absolutely foreign to the principles that govern the workings of a production process, is that one sows, another waters, another fertilizes, and another reaps: the mission, according to the Lord, is structured on the apostolic logic of continuity. In the Church, there are various ministries and charisms, and, if I may speak in these terms, apostolic success depends on every baptized person fully living his own vocation, doing what Jesus Christ has entrusted to him: if we are to sow, let us sow, trusting that others will water, others will fertilize, and others will reap.

I do not have the solution for so much failure in the transmission of the faith, but I am sure that the best "pastoral method" is that which is born of the wisdom of the *sentire cum Ecclesia* and then respects the principle that everyone involved can perform to the full extent of his abilities, without ever losing sight of the fact that, in the end, the principal actor is always the Lord with his grace. Especially today, when our societies are under the influence of such an aggressive laicism, the mission has to give priority to divine grace.

How does the work of the priest bear fruit? How does he generate hope and accompany individuals?

Certainly we have to focus on the "fruitfulness of the priest", especially now when many half-empty and aging parishes can dishearten the many priests who have given their all for the Lord.

Let us remember that Saint Paul presents himself as a father to believers (1 Thess 2:7, 11) and at the same time instructs Timothy regarding his relations with the elderly, telling him: "Do not rebuke an older man but exhort him *as you would a father;* treat younger men like brothers, older women like mothers, younger women like sisters, in all purity" (1 Tim 5:1–2 [emphasis added]). That is, the consecrated minister, seen as a father to the faithful who have been entrusted to his authority, is also called to behave almost like a son toward his elders, even lay persons, however strange this might seem from the point of view of human relationships.

At the level of grace, every priest, whether he is old or celebrating Mass for the first time, is called to exercise a "spiritual fatherhood". If a young parish vicar administers the anointing of the sick to a dying man or hears his confession, regardless of their age difference, in the relationship established between them the priest represents the fatherhood of God, his closeness and his mercy. The young, inexperienced priest becomes the father because he engenders divine life through the celebration of the sacraments, the preaching of the Word, and the exercise of his office as a pastor. The priest is always a father because he communicates life, especially through baptism, because he educates with the Word, because he offers nourishment in the Eucharist. He is a father because he is the channel for a divine benediction that passes through him from one generation of the baptized to another.

Certainly the fruitfulness of a priest, his ability to sow hope, will always have a close relationship to his personal maturity and how he lives his spiritual paternity through the sacrament and the Word. That spiritual paternity is a key factor on which depends the full realization, received as an unearned gift, of his vocation as a pastor, and he will be able to accompany with kindness and devotion, in the midst of many difficulties, the faithful who have been entrusted to him: this is called "pastoral charity". In doing so, whether the faithful are many or few, young or old, he will see with delight that the gift that they, too, receive fulfills its potential.

In that context, let us also talk about priestly celibacy, and specifically celibacy in the context of the priest's fatherliness. What is its significance?

Priestly celibacy, which is being challenged so much today in certain ecclesiastical quarters, is rooted in the Gospels as an evangelical counsel, but it also is intrinsically related to the ministry of the priest.

The priest is more than a religious functionary to whom has been attributed a mission that is independent of his life. His life is bound up in his apostolic mission, and therefore, very clearly in Saint Paul's thinking and also in the Gospels themselves, the evangelical counsel appears linked to the ministers chosen by Jesus. The apostles, in order to follow Christ, have left all human comforts behind, particularly their wives. In that connection, Saint Paul speaks to us about his own experience in 1 Corinthians 7:7, where he seems to consider celibacy to be a singular charism that he has received.

The link today between celibacy and the priesthood as a particular gift of God through which the holy ministers can unite themselves more easily and wholeheartedly to Christ (*CIC*, can. 277 §1; *Pastores dabo vobis*, no. 29) is found throughout the universal Church, though in various forms. In the Eastern Church, as we know, it affects only the priesthood of the bishops, but the very fact that it is required of them tells us that that Church does not conceive of it as an external discipline.

In the context of the response to celibacy mentioned above, the following analogy is widely used: a few years ago, it was unimaginable that a woman could be a soldier, and yet the modern armies of today have many women in their ranks who are fully capable of work that was traditionally considered to be exclusively for men. Will the same thing not happen with celibacy? Will it not be a deep-seated custom of the past that must be reconsidered? The substance of a soldier's profession, however, setting aside some questions of a practical nature, does not require the person who practices it to be of a particular sex, while the priesthood has an intimate connection with celibacy.

The documents of the Second Vatican Council and other, more recent magisterial documents teach a conformity or inner appropriateness between celibacy and the priesthood so that the Church of the Latin Rite does not feel itself empowered to change that doctrine with an arbitrary decision that breaks with the progressive development of centuries-long canonical regulation that began with a recognition of the interior link that preceded that regulation. We cannot break unilaterally from the series of declarations by a long line of popes and councils and from the steady and continuous adherence of the Catholic Church to the image of the celibate priest.

The crisis of celibacy in the Latin Catholic Church has been a recurring theme at particularly difficult moments in the Church. For example, we can evoke the days of the Protestant Reformation, those of the French Revolution, and more recently the years of the sexual revolution in the sixties and seventies of the last century. But if we can learn anything from studying these periods in the history of the Church and her institutions, it is that such crises have always demonstrated and consolidated the worth of the doctrine on celibacy.

There is no "probationary priesthood", just as there is no "probationary birth", no "probationary death", and no "probationary life". It seems today, however, that this truth is being obscured for various reasons: priestly failures, scandals, a scarcity of vocations . . . Can the institution of a "probationary priesthood" legitimately serve as a path to a solution of the crisis?

Absolutely not. It is a contradiction, a *contradictio in terminis*, as the Romans would say. Jesus came once and forever. He is a priest for all time, and those who act as ministers for the eternal Priest must show the conclusiveness of the salvation that Jesus Christ has earned for us. These ideas of a "probationary priesthood" are not in keeping with Jesus' mission.

A vocation is God's gift, and ordination is also his act: it is God, and not the priest, who makes him a priest. This calling, so demanding and so exceptional, requires the candidate before he is ordained to make a mature examination of himself, calmly and very strictly. He must know that his acceptance of lifelong consecration to the Lord is also an acceptance of the consequences that his ministry will entail in the future.

The now widespread idea of a "probationary priesthood" is characteristic of modernity, in which the general approach to an existence without God has occasioned a lack of faith in the perseverance of grace and, as a result, the emphasis on the fallible choice of man instead on the infallible choice of God. I repeat: it is a vocation that originates in the plan God has for me and that is sustained in his Divine Being, for since God is always faithful in his love, I can have complete trust that he will give me the grace I need to persevere in my mission until death. In fact, as the years go by, one discovers that, deep down, one becomes a priest, not for pleasure or because one will be happy that way or has made the decision on his own, but rather by the pure grace of God.

Another risk posed by growing secularization is the trap of functionalism, a phenomenon that can explain so many failures of vocation and proposals like those just mentioned. I would like to raise an example that I believe is enlightening: after the Second Vatican Council, it was decided that bishops over seventy-five years of age should immediately submit their resignations, and also priests older than seventy. But it was also decided that this modest change in the regulation of the practice of the priesthood should not be equated to actual retirement. In most cases, certainly, a bishop should withdraw because of age, as a function of his loss of physical or intellectual capacity, which could make it difficult or even impossible for him to practice his ministry. But age should not be the decisive criterion, because it involves more than assessing a functional competence in administering a sacrament that confers, in fact, a supernatural capacity. It will be said, correctly, that an eighty-year-old bishop cannot keep up the same pace in his work as a younger one, and it will also be said that it would be inconceivable not to establish a retirement age by law, but I do not believe that these are definitive arguments when aimed at the sacrament of ordination.

"Once a father, always a father." The sacrament of ordination establishes a new personal relationship, along the same lines as paternity, and therefore it is more than merely functional. A "probational priesthood" is not only self-contradictory, it shows a failure to understand the nature and substance of the sacramental priesthood of the Church.

This naturally raises the question of women in the priesthood, which has again been brought forward on various fronts today. Is it subject to review? Is it a disciplinary matter that the Church could simply change?

This is not a legitimate issue, because it touches on a subject that has already been decided. Pope Francis has made it clear, as have his predecessors: in that connection, I remember that Saint John Paul II, in number 4 of his Apostolic Exhortation *Ordinatio sacerdotalis* of 1994, reinforced with the use of the royal "we" ("*declaramus*"), the only document in which that pope uses that verb form, that it is a definitive doctrine infallibly taught by the ordinary universal Magisterium (*CIC*, can. 750 §2) that the Church does not have the authority to admit women to the priesthood. It is the province of the Magisterium to decide if a question is dogmatic or disciplinary: in this case, the Church has already decided that this proposition is dogmatic and that, because it is divine law, it cannot be changed or even reviewed. It can be supported with many reasons, such as fidelity to the example of the Lord or the normative nature of the centuries-old practice of the Church, but I do not believe this subject should be treated in depth here because the documents that gather the relevant considerations are sufficient explanation of the reasons for rejecting this possibility.

I would not want to leave it unsaid that there is an essential equality between male and female, in nature and also in the relationship with God through grace (see Gal 3:28). The priesthood, however, implies a sacramental symbolism of the relationship of Christ, the Head or husband, with the Church, the Body or wife. As it is, women can already discharge responsibility in the Church, with no problem at all: in that connection, whenever I can I make public my gratitude to the large group of women, both lay women and religious, some with university degrees, who lend their indispensable collaboration to the Congregation for the Doctrine of the Faith.

But, on the other hand, it would not be appropriate to make proposals *in merito* on the basis of simple human calculations, saying, for example, "if we open the priesthood to women, we will solve the vocational problem", or "if we were to accept the female priesthood, we would present a more modern image to the world." I think this is a very superficial, ideological, and above all anti-ecclesial way to frame the debate, because it sidesteps the fact that it involves a question of dogma that has already been resolved by the proper authority, and not one relating to a merely disciplinary subject.

You have just touched on the subject of vocations. Can we hope that a landowner will send more workers to work in his fields while the Western Church is in a state of decline? Would it not be better to seek another solution to the crisis in vocations, such as importing clergy or opening the priesthood to viri probati?

A vocational crisis cannot be dealt with by addressing only its symptoms and not its real cause. What has given rise to the vocational crisis? I believe I can say that it is a matter of a crisis of faith, which in turn is a result of a long secularization that has dried up what was once fertile soil and has scorched the earth. After all the damage, there is a lot of work to do! There is a lot of grain to be fertilized and many fields to return to and sow. But we must be careful with emergency solutions like shuffling vocations from one continent to another or one religious order to another, because these are often just patches and not real solutions, and frequently they also lack an evangelical foundation.

Are we aware that a massive inclusion of *viri probati*, which is especially foreseeable in countries where Catholicism is expanding and there are not many priests, would unquestionably mean the end of celibacy? But, in any case, what is the real problem? What do we need today? Do we need more Masses and, therefore, many *viri probati* who can celebrate them? Or do we need, instead, more committed and convinced faithful, who understand faith as a dedication to God in marriage, in religious life, in priestly consecration? What is the solution? Relativizing dedication? I believe not.

I am convinced that all of us must carry out a great process of inner conversion, spiritually renewing ourselves to adhere to God unconditionally. The present problem lies in the mediocrity of our ecclesial life and not in the absence of vocations for certain ministries. We cannot solve such big problems through compromise solutions or half-measures. Imagine a seminarian saying: "Yes, I want to work for the Church as a priest, but on the condition that I have a right to days off and retirement at sixty-five." For a priest, there is never a time when he "stops being a priest", the way a waiter or taxi driver stops being a waiter or taxi driver during his vacation. Of course, his legitimate sphere of privacy will always be respected, but he will never be able to say: "On such and such day of the week, I'll be free and won't be attending to the dying or celebrating Mass." If we are not truthful with this candidate for ordination, who is surely well intentioned but not yet very well educated—that is, if we do not tell him that his idea of a priest-functionary is completely the opposite of what Jesus wanted—we would be doing him a serious injustice.

The Church is the keeper of the depositum fidei. *Saint Paul was the first to use the image of a "deposit" in speaking about the treasure of faith, as a benefit that one has received and must care for and preserve. The image, despite all its misinterpretations, is magnificent: faith is a treasure, which we carry in earthen vessels. The question of "doctrine" should especially concern us on this point, particularly in this conversation with the Prefect of the Congregation for the Doctrine of the Faith. What is the relationship between doctrine and life? Is there such a thing as a doctrine that does not relate to a personal encounter, to a life? And, on the other hand, is there such a thing as a personal encounter or a life that does not involve or encompass doctrine? Is it conceivable in Christianity that there should be a scheme that begins with the personal encounter and then, as a further, secondary matter, ends with doctrine?*

This dichotomy is not valid, and it generates a good deal of confusion. Christian doctrine is not a theory, a system of the sort that idealism or even ideology offers—that is, a formulation of human ideas. If a man falls in love with a woman, he does not see that person as an example of a sociological theory of human relations! Christianity, for its part, has always given priority to the person over ideas, but when speaking of God, one must be careful not to let this prioritization drain doctrine of all its value.

God is truth, and the events in the story of salvation are a realization, under the conditions of concrete human history, of that truth which is God. I mean by this, among other things, that there is no element of doctrine that is outside a personal encounter, and vice versa. The God who forgives our sins, for example, is also the God whom we recognize in doctrine, in the confession of faith. We therefore cannot separate our faith in God as a person from the substance of the faith. God as a person, as truth, and as the substance of the confession of faith is absolutely one and the same. Nor can the truth of the faith be distinguished from the truth of morality relating to life, because God is at the same time both truth and goodness. The good God is the true God is the God of love: God is love (1 Jn 4:8).

Redemption is conditioned on orthodoxy, as is the correct conception of eternal life: orthodoxy is not just a theory about God, but a matter of God's personal relationship with me. For that reason, heresy always affects that personal relationship, because it separates God who is truth from the revelation of that same truth. For example, it would make no sense to say: "I believe in God, but I do not believe in God the Creator, because this attribute is a point of faith that was added after my personal encounter with God." Nor can I say, "I love Jesus, but I do not believe in the truth of the fact that Jesus is the Savior of all men, because that is something that has nothing to do with him as a person and was added later in theological thought."

The same thing happens when it comes to morality. I cannot say, "Lord, Lord", and not fulfill his will (see Mt 7:21). The Lord as a person is inseparable from the Lord as goodness. Orthodoxy is precisely participation in the act by which God knows himself in the Word and loves himself through the Spirit. In that way, orthodoxy and the upright and virtuous life are both the same participation in the intra-triune relations characteristic of divine life. Suppose I tell someone: "I have a good relationship with you, but I think you're a liar"; or I say I love a person and wish him well, but at the same time I allow myself to insult him. There would be a terrible contradiction between our personal relationship and my behavior toward those people. Something similar happens in the dichotomy that I mentioned before.

In that context, it seems to me that it would be relevant to mention the French philosopher Gabriel Marcel, because he reminds us that there is no human experience that does not carry with it a reflection about it—that is, the reflection is part of the experience itself. A poet does not first have the intuition and then adds words to it; he has the intuition with the words. Something similar applies to experience: it is an intuition with words that includes within it a first reflection. In that sense, can it be said that the formulas of faith are just "posterior reflection"? How should they be understood?

An encounter with God involves doctrine in an inseparable way. I hinted at this before, but I would like now to be
explicit about it: an encounter with Jesus is not empty and
content-free. Instead, it is an encounter with the Person of
the Son of God, which implies that in the encounter I am
confessing my faith in Jesus as the Son of God.

It is therefore a mistake to approach such a fundamental experience according to the logic of quantitative or
chronological/temporal concepts, as though doctrine were
an appendage to one's previous experience in life. In fact,
the content of faith is already present in the encounter and
makes it possible, so it does not appear afterward. Certainly, after the encounter I can have a better understanding or a more complete synthesis, I can reflect more deeply
on what has happened to me, but doctrine and confession
of faith, in themselves, are not that later reflection; instead,
they are the actual content of the encounter.

*A sociologist has spoken of a law within the revival of the religious
phenomenon as it is today: "a greater presence, at the expense of
fewer demands". It addresses an equation that is applicable to
all religions and points the way to success. As a result, some
people try to propose a "low-intensity Christianity". With this
approach, they say, Catholicism will be able to grow again in
numbers and social relevance: reducing content and requirements,
to put forth a Christianity more acceptable to all. Is this really a
proposition that would open the future and generate hope?*

I think not. Reduce God ... what can we say? Is it easier
to believe in two Divine Persons or in three? What would

this so-called lower intensity be? Christ would not be the Son of God, of the same substance as the Father? Christ would be just a prophet or a good man who has taught us to do good? Right there, this would not be a reduction: it would be a destruction!

The ways in which we present the truths of faith are quite another thing. We could certainly initiate people into the mysteries little by little, according to their capacity. Like Saint Paul, who explained the difference between adults in faith, who are ready for solid food, and children in faith, who must have milk. But teaching methods are one thing, and it is another, very different thing to change the content of faith.

We cannot think, for example, that if we were to reduce the intensity and demands of priestly life, there would be fewer defections and, perhaps, many would return to the ministry. No. What we really need is a complete renewal of each of us, as priests, to make it possible for young people to experience the beauty of ordained ministry, so that if they are candidates for the priesthood, they are educated well, with good theology and a profound spirituality, in the company of priests who set good examples. The solution, of course, will never be a sociological solution or a mere matter of pastoral organization. The cause of the crisis does not come from without or from mistaken ways of articulating the pastoral vocation: we would not gain much from better propaganda or promises of better living conditions or social relevance. Promising a young man that if he becomes a priest he will always have a good car, a good house, social recognition, further education ... These things are of no use in responding to such a substantial challenge!

For example, Catholic universities, like others, have gone from a certain elitism to a mass orientation. But

it is not a good solution to reduce the educational stan-
dards in order to attract more students. The university
is not just an institution of higher education. To attain
academic excellence and instill passion in the students for
the "culture of life, the culture of truth" (Benedict XVI,
Lecture for Delivery at the Sapienza University of Rome), the
solution lies in a general renewal, in finding good profes-
sors who identify with what they are teaching, in inviting
students to take maximum advantage of the time they
have for study in university, which will not be easy to
come by during the rest of their lives. In the same way,
we need priests who do not have the mentality of func-
tionaries and who are not always looking for ploys to
justify the Church's existence in a secular society, almost
as though they were apologizing. They should know
that they have to guide men and women who have been
strongly secularized at the hands of the prevailing ideologies, lost sheep without a shepherd, who live in ambiv-
alence, who live among existential questions that they
do not even want to formulate because they know the
answers might trouble them.

Amid so much irrationality and frivolity, we must seek
out the enemy—nihilism, agnosticism, and skepticism, so
widespread in our society because of its loss of realism and
humanity—and, with the help of the riches of the Magisterium of the Church, fight it systematically. Everything is
reinvented, anything goes. In society, we can only expect
the wind that blows us this way and that. In society, we
can only seek the comfort of being always on the side of
the majority and not that of the brave witness we bear by
swimming against the current when we must.

I would like to bring up here an attestation I read not
long ago that moved me profoundly: Ernst Nolte (*Contro-
versy: National Socialism, Bolshevism, the Jewish Question in*

the History of the Nineteenth Century) has affirmed recently that the Holy Office, which is today the Congregation for the Doctrine of the Faith, was in 1940 the only recognized institution in the whole world that expressly condemned "the annihilation of life unworthy of life". We belong to this sometimes sinful Church, but she is usually glorious in her defense of life and the human, as Saint John Paul II often emphasized. This saint understood and therefore taught that the key for our world is to further the encounter between Christ and the heart of man: when man is again of God and for God, he finds human existence's reason for being on earth. As he said to the university students in 1978, the Christian faith is what best enables us to interpret the deepest aspects of the human being.

We cannot and should not mince our words. This reminds me of the episode of Peter's denials, when they say to him while he is waiting in the Praetorium, "Your accent gives you away." But he denies and denies again that he is part of Jesus' group. We, too, must speak this same dialect, this Christian language, without fear of being given away by it. Christians, when we are being Christians, speak differently! It is necessary that people realize it: this is our language, full of the Holy Spirit. Let us be recognized as speaking the language of the Spirit of Christ!

Let me pose at exactly this juncture a question about truth. It is about the sentence, "Who am I to judge?" These words of Pope Francis, taken out of context and applied as though they were a general rule, have sometimes been cited as a change in direction toward a more open, less dogmatic Christianity. "From anathema sit to 'Who am I to judge?'" Is this a real change of direction? And, going deeper, what authority does the Church, or an individual Christian, have to judge personal situations?

It is precisely those who before have shown no respect for the doctrine of the Church who now seize on a stray sentence of the Holy Father, taken out of context, to present deviant ideas about sexual morality in the guise of a presumed interpretation of the "authentic" thought *in merito* of the pope.

The homosexual issue that gave rise to the question asked of the Holy Father already appears in the Bible, both in the Old Testament (see Gen 19; Deut 23:18f.; Lev 18:22, 20:13; Wis 13–15) and in the Pauline letters (Rom 1:26f.; 1 Cor 6:9f.), treated as a theological subject (with the appropriate conditions entailed with the historicity of revelation). The concept of the intrinsic disorder of homosexual acts, because they do not proceed from a genuine emotional and sexual complementarity, stems from Holy Scripture. It involves a very complex question, because of the many implications that have emerged so forcefully in the last few years. In any case, the anthropological conception that is derived from the Bible carries with it some inescapable moral exigencies and, at the same time, a scrupulous respect for the homosexual person. Such persons, called to chastity and Christian perfection through self-mastery, sometimes supported by a disinterested friendship, live an authentic "trial. They must be accepted with respect, compassion, and sensitivity. Every sign of unjust discrimination in their regard should be avoided" (*Catechism of the Catholic Church*, nos. 2357–59).

But beyond the problem raised by the decontextualization of Pope Francis' sentence mentioned above, uttered as a sign of respect for personal dignity, it seems evident to me that the Church, with her Magisterium, has the power to judge the morality of specific situations. This is an undisputed truth: God is the only judge who will judge us at the end times, and the pope and bishops have the obligation to present the revealed criteria for this Last Judgment which our moral conscience already anticipates. The Church has always said "this is true, this is false", and no one can live by his own subjectivist interpretation of God's commandments, the Beatitudes, the councils, according to his own criteria, his interest, or even his needs, as if God were merely a backdrop to his autonomy. The relationship between personal conscience and God is concrete and real, illuminated by the Magisterium of the Church; the Church has both the right and the obligation to declare that a doctrine is false, precisely because that doctrine diverts ordinary people from the road that leads to God.

Ever since the French Revolution and during the successive liberal regimes and then the totalitarian rule of the twentieth century, the object of the most important attacks has always been the Christian conception of human existence and its destiny. When Christianity's resistance could not be overcome, some of its elements were allowed to continue, but not the substance of Christianity. As a result, it ceased to be the criterion of all reality, and the subjectivist positions mentioned above gained favor.

They originated in a new, non-Christian, relativist anthropology that dispenses with the concept of truth: today's man feels obligated to live in perennial doubt. What is more, the affirmation that the Church cannot judge personal situations is based on a false soteriology, that is, that man is his own savior and redeemer. Subjecting Christian anthropology to this brutal reductionism, the hermeneutics of reality that derives from it adopts only those elements that are in the interest of or convenient for the individual: some elements of the parables, some kind gestures of Christ, or those passages that would present him as a simple prophet of social matters or a master in humanity. The Lord of history is censored out, as is the Son of God who invites us to conversion and the Son of

Man who will come to judge the living and the dead. In reality, this Christianity, merely tolerated, is left empty of its message, forgetting that, without personal conversion, a relationship with Christ is impossible.

This situation which we have described, this question about hope in the Church, takes us back to the subject of Vatican II. What we have experienced in these last few months almost seems like a déjà vu of what we saw in the years after that council. Voices have emerged that see the present ecclesial period as a return to the problems of those days. Basically, it has been said that two big problems have appeared: the relationship between the Church and the world and the relationship between the Spirit and the Word. Do you think this analysis is correct?

Pope Francis is insisting to us that the Church should not be self-referential, always talking about herself. With respect to the sign of salvation that has already been given, it seems to me more important to talk about people's desire to encounter Jesus and the gift that doing so gives man today than it is to waste too much time focusing on ourselves.

We also have to bear in mind that some past issues have been theologically overcome. When Pope Benedict XVI explained the relationship between the "Jesus of history" and the "Jesus of faith" in his book *Jesus of Nazareth*, he addressed the relationship between Spirit and Word. The unnatural division between the Jesus of history and the Jesus of faith underlies the division between Spirit and Word, while there is no real contradiction between the historical and spiritual dimensions of faith, between the acts of Christ who was born, died, and resurrected in the flesh and the permanent action of the Spirit in believers. This problem is, or at least should be, one that has already been solved.

It is true, however, that after the council many people expected a new springtime for the Church, and instead, in some respects, it seems as though what came was a deep winter. Is it accurate to speak of a "postconciliar crisis" in the Church?

Despite the much-proclaimed "postconciliar crisis", I believe it would be more accurate to speak of a "preconciliar crisis". In saying that, I want to affirm clearly and bluntly that the cause of the current crisis of faith is not to be found in the council as such: all its documents, in all their richness, present the Christian faith in its entirety! Think of the great constitutions: *Dei verbum*, which addresses magisterially the great subject of the Word of God in the Church; *Lumen gentium*, on the Church, the people of God, and the Body of Christ; or the prophetic, realistic, and profoundly hopeful vision for today's world that is *Gaudium et spes*. If they are read and studied with care, these can never lead us to the idea that they are the cause of the crisis in faith we are sketching out here. The council not only bore great fruit for the Church at a very complicated time, it also gathered together the best of the biblical, liturgical, and patristic movements that preceded it, inaugurating a wholly new ecclesiological line from which we will be able to imbibe for many decades.

What happened, then? Where should we look for the causes of this "crisis"?

We have to go back to the Enlightenment to understand the great challenges that face the Church, left unresolved by the Second Vatican Council, which have a notable philosophical dimension.

Kant's theory of knowledge denied, or at least relativized, the possibility of metaphysical knowledge. In the end, it also denied that the foundation of theology was science. When, ideologically, empirical proof became the only criterion of truth, it produced a surprising reductionism in the horizon of the knowledge of God as a reality independent of ourselves. If God is simply a moral postulate, an ideal, or a postulate of practical reason, then God depends on the finite knowledge of man. These principles, affirmed by this great philosophical current, ran up against metaphysical postulates, which took as their starting point the independent existence of God.

We need a philosophy of reality and of being. A philosophy in which the thinking man reaches the point where he can say: "God exists. Perhaps I do not know him as such, as a personal being, but I know he exists." Only then will man be open to the possibility that God will reveal himself historically and that, through his Word, he makes himself accessible in language, thought, and human acts.

Could you explain a little more the immediate origin of this "preconciliar crisis"?

Yes. Ultimately, I believe I can detect a great point of conflict between the historical positivist method and all the philosophical reflection regarding the being of things, that is, the metaphysical vision of reality. It is a key point that already appears within the framework of the Protestant exegesis at the end of the nineteenth century, with the opposition between the "Jesus of history" and the "Jesus of faith" to which I referred before. Friedrich Schleiermacher long ago arrived at a solution to these questions that has been shown to be absolutely inadequate. He proposed a philosophy of Christianity in which the dogma of the Church, which is to say the confessed faith, was just a theoretical expression and practice of a religious sentiment of dependence on the Absolute. This theologian thus founded a "Protestantism of culture" that, following Adolf von Harnack, had a great influence on some Catholic theologians like Alfred Loisy: in fact, its influence extended to the entire current that in the Catholic Church was called "modernism", which germinated especially at the end of the nineteenth century and the beginning of the twentieth.

Modernity has consisted of an objective, programmed, and censorious secularization (Jean Daniélou, *Church and Secularization*) that, from the starting point of a first ambiguous affirmation in the early Middle Ages of the principle of the autonomy of man and passing through a rationalism that made the scientific-mathematical method absolute, has arrived at the optimistic affirmation of the full autonomy of temporal reality and, therefore, of purely natural man, who attains self-realization with his own intelligence and his own will.

Modernism is the ecclesial current that uncritically accepts the postulates of modernist thought, attempting thereby to resize itself in a world that is moving farther and farther away from the Church. Founded on a flawed theology of revelation and the dogmatic transmission of faith, modernism reduced reason to rationalism and belief in Christ to subjectivism, privatizing faith to the point of making it irrelevant to the world and abandoning a vigorous discourse about the truth in favor of a discourse on praxis. A Christianity that does not need the holiness that is Christ's gift through the Church did not need to be propagated, either, so the mission, to the extent that it went beyond the promotion of all that is human, was understood as useless proselytism that was offensive to the liberty and dignity of others. In that connection, we should note the repeated contemporaneous attempts to find a common moral denominator based on universal solidarity and brotherhood. My humble opinion is that the genesis of the great crisis of faith that came at the Second Vatican Council is this conception of man as being radically self-sufficient and autonomous. A crisis of faith that, above all, has been a profound crisis of Christian hope. It is for that reason that I prefer to use the term "preconciliar crisis".

From these postulates we can also explain, for example, the great liturgical crisis. The wavering over the concept of the revelation and existence of God, of historical revelation and Christological dogma, sapped the power of the liturgy, because it is the personal encounter with God and not an encounter between man and himself, with his feelings and desires. The Catholic liturgy has been reduced so many times to a game about symbols or an instrument of consolation whenever it is needed, when a vague religious sentimentalism or a mere moral or social exhortation has not worked.

In the face of certain attacks by some fundamentalists and those who suffer from nostalgia for a reality that in any case has never existed, we must declare plainly that Christian fragmentation is rooted in the preconciliar crisis. The process of the disintegration of faith, through the design of a Christianity lite that reduced it to a sentimental-emotional level, a politico-supportive level, and little more, had already been set in motion decades before the Second Vatican Council. In that connection, I would like here to vindicate the great figure of Pius XI, the pope who best understood the disastrous cultural project of the secularist mentality and who laid the groundwork for an effective counterattack through a Magisterium that understands that it is responsible for a great tradition and is daring and proactive.

Although in Western countries the symptoms had not emerged in all their harshness and many people still practiced religion and there were many vocations, what was already clear was the loss of the working world and the world of culture for the sake of an "immanentism" in which all reality had lost its point of reference to the transcendent. Pope Pius XI, who was ahead of his time in correctly interpreting the contemporary ideological currents in their various combinations and took specific and effective action to confront them, prepared the ground for a reaction that would take concrete shape decades later.

The great lesson that we can learn from that today, on the fiftieth anniversary of the end of the Second Vatican Council, is that when an anthropology founded on revelation is abandoned, man sees himself as a mere phenomenon of evolution, which then becomes the fundamental paradigm that supplants the metaphysics of being and reality. Once everything has been reduced to the immanent by an elitist culture, supported by academia and the mass media, man does not need his history, starts to believe in the permanent revolution that permits him to reinvent everything over and over, until he finally becomes the manipulable object that the powers that be have always wanted. In that connection, consider how the state has become, progressively and almost without restraint, the center, the guarantor, and the generator of all social life. We therefore must accept that the Christian presence in today's world, when its educational role is not accepted, is one of either resistance or martyrdom.

I imagine that this "immanentism" that you just described has other very real-world consequences; can you name some of them?

Gender ideology very clearly develops out of this logic. This ideology aims to inculcate in us the idea that there is nothing in human nature that determines whether a person is a man or a woman, so that sexual identity is a personal option that depends on one's own desire. The body stops being the place where one meets God the Creator and becomes a kind of machine that I can mold, adjust, and use as I like, answering only to myself and my feelings.

You can see another example in the culture that has grown up around the fact of death. Because we no longer expect the resurrection of the body and we think that all our reality unfolds between the walls of this world, we try to erase all reference to the hereafter and every sign of hope in everything that surrounds our personal death. How sad it is when, in the "lay" funeral, one does not hear a single word of the Bible or see a single sign of the cross, the saints, or the history of salvation. Ashes are scattered in inappropriate places, such as under a tree or in the sea, with the pretense of thereby fostering the memory of the loved one when, actually, what we are doing is casting him into the most dehumanizing and humiliating anonymity. Not to mention the ridiculous childishness with which we talk about the death of loved ones to our children or how we encourage the importation into our schools of strange customs, foreign to our own tradition, such as Halloween. With actions such as these, the Christian meaning of death is irremediably lost and, with it, all possibility of true consolation with which to bear the heavy burden of being separated from a loved one.

It is not hard to see how the concepts of rationalism and immanentism make their way into actual life and daily practice, our feelings, our life-style, poetic expression, the great works of literature or films or art ... In the same vein, consider how the artistic styles of the avant-garde favor the impersonal, shapes without face or form, in which we can identify no one by his face, his name, or his sex ... Everything is represented as a fluid, undifferentiated, amorphous phenomenon ... This art, as a child of its time, captures the idea that there is no essence of man or of things that would at the same time be an expression of participation in the being of the Creator, in his creative ideas, in his salvific will, in his love.

Christianity has a positive conception of reality that is very different: the good orients and directs being. Understood correctly, it involves going beyond the immanentism that is typical of many exponents of contemporary philosophy, like Schleiermacher, already mentioned, who bases everything on the "feeling of dependence on God". This feeling is, basically, a humiliating feeling, as if the relationship with God were founded only on the fact that I depend on him. Christianity begins instead with the recognition of a belonging to God that means "being at God's side". The contingency of man thus does not resolve itself into a simple feeling of dependence on God, a simple comparison between absolute being and relative being. The creation, the first revelation of God's love, is what founds and sustains the opening of all existence to God.

Man is therefore open to God insofar as he is rational. Through reason he can know God in his Being, in his divinity, that is, in the love that is the foundation of the *bonum*, the goodness of everything that God has created. It is in this metaphysical dimension that we must put moral law in context: it is not a collection of positive orders. On the contrary, the commandments express the salvific will of God and are in man's conscience as a first self-revelation of God's goodness there. Natural law, which is today so reviled and even caricatured, is not a bio-empirical law, that is, the description of the empirical bio-animal nature of man. Instead, it refers principally to his relational nature, in which his corporeality and the accompanying inclinations all possess an intrinsic rationality. Natural law is founded on the *logos* with which God has stamped man.

We agree, then, on the very great weight we must give to this "preconciliar crisis". In any case, I would like to know your perspective on the great diminution in vocations, and in the practice of the Catholic religion in general, that has characterized the whole postconciliar period, at least in the Western countries. In that connection, are they purely collateral effects?

They certainly are very negative effects. But in any case, it is not possible to speak in terms of a shipwreck of the postconciliar Church, as some do. It would perhaps be better to speak in terms of a strong storm, at most. But, to continue with the simile, in the middle of the waves that break against our ship, threatening to capsize it, Jesus is always there, the only one who can calm the menacing winds (see Mt 14:24–32). It is up to us whether we flee the ship in fear or stay on board, entrusting ourselves to Jesus and fighting to keep the vessel afloat in the hope that the storm will abate. Anyone who has lived through that has understood perfectly the only way open to genuine spiritual reform of the Church. It is no coincidence, therefore, that in the Apostolic Palaces of the Vatican or in the Basilica, the scene of Jesus calming the storm is repeated relatively frequently (see, for example, the *Navicella* of Giotto, ca. 1300, on the internal wall of the atrium of the Basilica), as though signaling to the Holy Father and his close collaborators in the Curia the only one in whom they must place all their trust.

In reality, the only possible way to overcome the negative elements that you have just enumerated, it seems to me, is to analyze and take note of what happened in the Reformation of the sixteenth century. The Church suffered a great crisis then, too, and in fact it appeared as though Catholicism were going to disappear from Europe. How did it recover? With a healthy and clear doctrine and with good pastors, like Saint Charles Borromeo and many other great bishops and parish priests in the path laid out by the Tridentine Reform. Moreover, notice that, to convince the people, they did not predominantly use powerful political tools but, rather, humble example and faith. I believe that here we have the two keys to overcoming this crisis: on the one hand, living the religious life and priesthood seriously and demandingly; on the other, educating our youth in generosity, within the nucleus of strong families, recognizing them as having priority in the education of their children.

In that connection, let us remember that the great totalitarianisms have always attempted to take away from the family this fundamental right to educate their children: the Komsomol, the Hitler-Jugend, the Opera Balilla are three clear examples of how these ideologies had understood that the family and its great defender, the Church, were the institutions that most resisted the social disintegration they wanted to impose.

Just as in the time of the Tridentine Reform there was a whole series of great theologians who helped the Church find her way to her cultural response, so there was at the time of Vatican II ...

Of course, some theologians contributed a great deal, and with great acuity, to deepening the openness to the revelation that I mentioned earlier of the postulates of fundamental theology and philosophy of being. I am thinking especially of Karl Rahner, in his great work *Hearer of the Word*, and of other authors who have made it possible to present a new fundamental theology transcending the pure phenomenology of religion, on the order of a metaphysics of the existence of God. Here, it is a matter, not just of presenting a series of religious phenomena, but rather of reaching the real as the foundation of those phenomena. This meant going beyond the rationalism, the empiricism, the positivism of the nineteenth century—that is, the great causes of the crisis of faith. In that connection, I always recommend studying the work of Henri de Lubac, particularly his book *The Drama of Atheist Humanism*.

The Second Vatican Council has been defined as a "pastoral council". But what is pastoral? Pastoral activities and programs? Advice and structure? If what is pastoral consists of the deeds of the Good Shepherd, should it not be seen as being in intimate relation with the sacraments, with the life communicated in them? Would this not make all of the Church's actions pastoral? How can we get beyond a vision that sterilizes the ministry of the priest because it sets the pastoral against dogma or law or the institution?

This insistence on calling Vatican II a "pastoral council", and therefore Trent a "dogmatic council", is more a journalistic expression than a theological one. Ecumenical councils take as their subject matter all the issues and the whole life of the Church: elements that are dogmatic, pastoral, liturgical ... everything in the life of the Church. In this sense, we can say, too, that the Council of Nicaea was very pastoral, because if Jesus Christ was not the true Son of God, consubstantial with the Father, neither would the salvation of man or the action of the Good Shepherd be possible. Christ is the Good Shepherd because he is the Word of God incarnate, the Son of God come into this world. For that reason we can say that Nicaea, the great supposedly "dogmatic" council, was actually a profoundly "pastoral" one.

It is true that Vatican II did not propose to condemn particular heresies that denied an article of faith. But, in a broad sense, the council did systematically take up and condemn the most pernicious heresies of our time, such as rationalism or the reduction of revelation to a moral or sentimental religious system. It also refuted and rejected that pan-naturalist anthropology that, from a reductionist evolutionism, argues that man is no more than a mere animal. It also condemned the current pernicious heresy that presents the liturgy as a system of self-referential symbols.

The council did formulate its rejection of these cultural forms, not as a contradiction, but as an advance beyond them. It went on ahead of these ideas. Its rejection was not presented as opposition but, rather, as a proposition. Its explanation invoked the gospel, explaining it as a unit, in its entirety, within the context of the Church's mission. It is therefore not legitimate to relativize the Second Vatican Council by saying that it was a mere pastoral council. We have, as we often do, two extremes: the position of some traditionalists, who relativize the council because it was not dogmatic, and the position of the modernists, who interpreted this ecclesial event as a final stage of the modern self-definition of the Church, which in a certain way superseded the apostolic tradition. As if the Church, understood within the limits of immanentism and rationalism, could define herself like any other organization.

But let us return to your question. The pastoral approach is not just a technique for organizing something, for entertaining people, for attracting or distracting them. The pastoral approach comes from Jesus, who is the Good Shepherd. It should always take him as its point of departure and therefore should take individuals, and their search for the true and the good, seriously. The true pastoral approach is based on the knowledge that the truth, in capital letters, is the only thing that can satisfy them and fulfill their desire. The truth should be the starting point of all pastoral action.

The pastoral actions that a pastor proposes are, first and foremost, the sacraments, and most especially the Eucharist. It is not an agenda designed to entertain people in their free time or a psychologist who is there to propose activities that amuse and entertain the children and young people who go to weekly catechism. In emulation of the Good Shepherd, it pervades the fabric of people's lives, their conflicts and concrete difficulties, their families, their work, their relationships. A priest, having been given responsibility for healing their souls, knows that it is in the Eucharist that people's whole life is put in play, because it is the same life that is offered in its entirety "for all men", as a sacrifice that binds one to Christ.

A seasoned and responsible pastor knows that, above all, he must be careful and solicitous in preparing Holy Mass, especially in the decorum of the celebration and preaching of Sunday Mass, which should offer true nourishment and not theological or exegetical theories that may seem enlightening but actually are interesting to no more than a few, apart from the preacher. The good pastor preaches Christ and offers him, with the greatest seemliness, in the bloodless sacrifice of the Mass. This should be the constant point of reference for everything pastoral and the fundamental norm that should animate the special vigilance incumbent on bishops over the pastoral behavior developed in their respective dioceses.

In this context of sacraments and the pastoral, the question also arises about the life that Christianity communicates through the revealed Word. Specifically, what can we hope for from the Gospels? Can I really hope that they will speak to me today? Would

this not be an exaggerated expectation? Would it not be better to
approach these texts with the eye of a historian, in the best sense,
to be sure—that is, the historian who seeks to learn from the past
and is a great admirer of the Jesus of history?

The historical-critical method serves to deepen our understanding of the history of salvation and the revelation of
God through history. This method has a certain utility,
because it does not pose any intellectual obstacle to the
faith of those who want to believe. But one must keep
in mind that the evangelists bore witness in writing to
what they had seen and heard, not by neutrally describ-
ing external facts, but rather by realizing a living confession of faith—that is, representing the mystery of the
Person of Jesus. He appeared then, not as just another
prophet, but as the Son of God, who had a fundamental,
eternal relationship with the Father and a historical, concrete, filial relationship with him.

The books of the Old and New Testaments were written so that we could realize the act of faith and believe
in Jesus Christ. The act of faith is, therefore, a personal
encounter that transcends the empirical realm of history
and the methods of the historian. This does not mean
that we should fall into a new dualism or fideism: thinking of faith as a personal encounter with Christ does not
mean contrasting the historical facts of faith with its subjective interpretations. The historical facts and personages
of revelation, like the prophets and the apostles, carry in
themselves this message of the revelation of God in Jesus
Christ. Therefore, though we cannot prove the divinity of Jesus empirically, there is nothing to prevent us
from believing that, through his history and humanity,
God himself wanted to reveal himself and that through
the humanity of Jesus God reveals his Son's eternal relationship with the Father and the Holy Spirit. The key

here is to understand the definitive revelation of God the Father, Son, and Holy Spirit recounted in the life, death, and Resurrection of Jesus. Holy Scripture is the written witness of this revelation.

Yes, the Church also offers us Holy Scripture as a repository of hope. Saint Augustine says: "Truly, I would not believe the Gospel if the authority of the Catholic Church did not move me to do so." How then should we interpret Holy Scripture? Here we come up against a question that is key for theology and the Christian life. Interpreting Holy Scripture in the Church: What does that mean? Eckhart Reinmuth recently said in a book on the hermeneutics of the New Testament: "The texts of the New Testament did not require their readers to start from any special or exclusive premise in order to understand them: they spoke in the language of their world, of their time. Understanding the New Testament today therefore can, all the more, necessitate a renunciation of all sorts of protective walls of that kind. In a very precise sense, the New Testament can be read without any premise at all." Which obviously prompts the question whether there is a "premise" when approaching the New Testament. Is it a "neutral" book, open to any reading?

In the wake of the great discussions over the last three hundred years regarding the interpretation of Scripture, the idea of an unprejudiced reading certainly sounds somewhat ingenuous. Our response to this great challenge of interpretation should match the level of the preceding discussion. One does not normally come to Jesus after a single reading of a single book or of something written two thousand years ago. Today one reads Holy Scripture—the Old and New Testaments—because one knows, even without being a Christian, that it is the religious book of the Church. The intimate connection of the Church with the Bible—that is, of the communion of believers in Christ with the book that contains the apostolic testimony of Jesus as Christ and the Son of God—is undeniable.

The writings of the Church express her faith. For that reason, the historical-critical method cannot claim to be a unique neutral reading of the Bible. In fact, our acceptance of faith does not begin with an exact reconstruction of the historical situation of the time described by the texts: faith always depends on an encounter with the risen Christ, and this comes thanks to the uninterrupted witness borne by the Church since the time of the apostles. Their personal testimony situates us in the Church, in her life and her mystery. We in the community of the baptized can recognize that the evangelical writings of the apostles are really offering a living witness to the mystery and message of the person who was Jesus. But faith, considered in itself, does not begin in the book as such.

The evangelist Luke speaks to us about just this reality in his introduction to the Gospel. He says there that he is writing to the "most excellent" Theophilus "that you may know the truth concerning the things of which you have been informed" (Lk 1:3–4). First comes the witness and the catechesis, the received teaching—that is, the tradition. Only after that, with the texts that the evangelist wrote and in the context of a community of faith, can the Christian personally affirm his own.

And the cultural differences between the two periods? Based on what premises can we adjust for the distance in time and culture that characterizes the Gospels?

All the texts of the New Testament speak in the language of their time, framed in the cultural categories of their time. But that language and those cultural categories do not get in the way of the dialogues between the different historical eras, because they refer to human experiences that are similar to ours. Let us pick an example that will help us understand better: the tools used in the harvesting of wheat were different in Jesus' day, yet today, too, we know when we eat bread that we need wheat and that wheat has to be sown, grown, and reaped. The forms vary, but not the basic, original experiences. Another example: the political forms may vary in the government of a country, but not the fact that men are social beings who seek to organize themselves as a society.

Man has always asked himself fundamental questions about the meaning of death, the search for truth, respect for moral values, and the measure of the human being ... What do we need today in order to find Jesus Christ through biblical witness? Certainly, it is not a closed philosophical system or hermeneutics, such as empiricism or idealism, which hinder the acceptance of revealed truth. God cannot depend on a particular hermeneutic theory.

We need, instead, an open mind that recognizes the principles of thought and good conduct, not in subjective categories, but in the basic elements of knowing reality through the *analogia entis*, which is the grammar of revelation, thereby to understand the language in which God speaks to us, always and in every era. Being, the good, the dignity of the person, relationships among people, the family, these are the grammatical structures that make it possible to understand Scripture. It is this "grammar of creation" that makes it possible for God to reveal himself, in the history of man and to man.

We are seeing with some concern the attempt to reduce exegesis to the knowledge of certain technical aspects that sometimes bear very little relevance. For example, if I want to understand the episode of the Gerasene demoniac and the two thousand swine that rushed down the steep bank into the sea, the biology of swine will matter very little to me, as will the angle of the incline and the temperature of the water. I know that the point of the story is something else. That is, I do not need to know all the historical, scientific, or cultural circumstances in order to understand the biblical text. Let us imagine, to cite another example, the story of the Flood and the saving of Noah and his family in the ark. The matter of whether it is possible for a wooden ark to endure such a storm or the meteorological conditions in the story do have a certain interest but little relevance. What the text tells us is that when man distances himself from God, everything ends in chaos, while if he places his hope in divine aid, it will not be disappointed. This is the message. In any case, the value of a tale like that of the Flood is not the same as the value of the true story of the death and Resurrection of the body of Christ, as it is recounted in the Gospels. In a sound exegesis, certain elements and aspects can hold some interest, but the key must be to seek an understanding of the message or point of the story in question.

It would seem to an outside observer that the differences between the Catholic Church and other Christian confessions are not really all that important. They could be seen as theological minutiae that matter to specialists but not to the ordinary person. If so, it would seem better to focus ecumenism on cooperation in charity and social service, make gestures that end old differences, and forget about abstract arguments. These are matters that have been on the table for a long time now. What would you say about this? Does this point of view not reflect an underappreciation of the question of truth, so characteristic of the postmodern culture and so foreign to the Christian perspective, in which Jesus manifests himself as the Truth in person?

The farther away an observer is from Christianity, the fewer differences he can see between the Catholic Church and the other Christian denominations. To an atheist, all religions look the same. To a believer with a hazy religious sensibility for an impersonal expression of the mystery— that is, for a reality beyond everyday phenomena or even beyond the difference between being and not being—all the religions that profess a personal God appear the same; at most they would be different ways of adoring the only God. To the liberal, modernist Christian, who sees nothing more in faith than a cultural phenomenon, the apologetic teachings and doctrinal differences among the various confessions seem like nothing but the rigid expression of a kind of "partisan spirit" and an apodictic comprehension of the truth, which in itself cannot be recognized. This Christian's reasoning is: Just as the transcendental *ego* would not be capable of comprehending reality, the thing in itself, except by its shape and appearance from intuitions and categories, so the religious *ego* would recognize in the revealed Word, not God, but rather human ideas of the divine, which may reflect the mystery in its multiple facets but certainly cannot express it with adequate clarity through the profession of faith and dogma.

The relativism characteristic of the postmodernism that you mention in your question makes a radical mistake in presuming to say that the truth cannot be known. Because, together with the act of knowing, there is also the ontological and epistemological test for distinguishing true knowledge from false knowledge. Similarly, the theory that postulates that renouncing the possibility of knowing the truth favors a more tolerant coexistence contradicts our experience; it turns out, instead, that the vacuum that that renunciation creates, regarding fundamental questions about God, the world, and the human being, is filled by political and philosophical ideologies of a totalitarian nature, which, by renouncing truth, automatically disable human freedom.

A realistic focus on the world and the fundamental questions of our existence allows us to say that the human being is absolutely capable of knowing the truth that is manifested to him by the being of things and of being attracted by their goodness, so that on the basis of the very existence of the world, he can rise rationally to the certainty of being and the power of God (see Rom 1:8). Man is called, therefore, to hear a revelation in which God manifests himself to him in the Word and the Spirit. Through the creation and the Incarnation, man enters sacramentally into a community of salvation with God, in person and in dialogue.

This knowledge is common to all those who accept that Jesus Christ, the Son of God, assumed our humanity. But differences of opinion about the historical mediation, through grace, of the truth and life that Jesus Christ has brought us are not therefore relegated to secondary status. Ecumenical theology, for example, has this reality as a goal—that is, how to attain a common understanding of the sacramental and hierarchic constitution of the Church, of her effective signs of salvation, of the apostolic tradition, and of her infallible Magisterium.

In 2017 we will have the quincentennial, which Catholics and Protestants will observe together, of the beginning of Luther's reform. In that way some common act of memorialization will be wanted, to reach a shared view of history that permits reconciliation. Some might see in such an act, however, a relativization

*of the differences between Catholicism and the Protestant confes-
sions. The German theologian Karl-Heinz Menke has recently
written a book in which he states that, in spite of many years
of dialogue, the great differences—precisely those regarding the
sacramental vision of the Church and the world—persist and are
even deepening. Menke cites some examples of how these differences translate into practice: the ordination of women to the priesthood, the promotion of a "Church from below", or the pressure
to share the Eucharist among different confessions. To these may
be added the fact that many Protestant confessions have effusively
embraced gender ideology. Can pressure on the Church to accept
these changes, coming from the media, be seen as a Protestantization of Catholicism?*

This anniversary should be an occasion for all Christians,
including Catholics, to reflect, to undertake an examination
of conscience regarding the causes of the Reformation at the
time, and even to embark on a new ecumenical dialogue.
Strictly speaking, we Catholics do not have any reason to
celebrate October 31, 1517, the date that is considered
to be the beginning of the Reformation that led to the rup-
ture in Western Christianity. If we are convinced that revelation has been preserved, in its entirety and unchanged,
through Scripture and tradition in the doctrine of the faith,
in the sacraments, in the hierarchic constitution of the
Church by divine right, founded on the sacrament of holy
orders, we cannot accept that there are sufficient reasons to
separate from the Church.

The members of the Protestant ecclesial communities
see this event from another perspective, because they think
it is the appropriate occasion for celebrating the rediscovery
of the "pure word of God", which has been presumably
disfigured throughout history by merely human traditions.
The Protestant reformers concluded five hundred years ago

that some hierarchies of the Church not only were morally corrupt but had distorted the gospel and, as a result, had blocked believers' path of salvation to Jesus Christ. To justify the separation, they accused the pope, presumed to be the head of this system, of being the Antichrist.

How can we realistically make progress today in the ecumenical dialogue with the evangelical communities? The theologian Karl-Heinz Menke is right when he says that the relativization of the truth and the uncritical adoption of modern ideologies are the main obstacle to unity in the truth. In this sense, a Protestantization of the Catholic Church based on secular thought without reference to transcendence cannot reconcile us with the Protestants or even allow an encounter with the mystery of Christ, for in him we are depositaries of a supernatural revelation to which we all owe complete obedience of our intellect and will (see *Dei verbum*, no. 5).

I believe that the Catholic principles of ecumenism, as they were proposed and developed by the decree of the Second Vatican Council, continue to be in full effect (see *Unitatis redintegratio*, nos. 2–4). In any case, I believe the document of the Congregation for the Doctrine of the Faith *Dominus Iesus*, of the holy year 2000, misunderstood by many and unjustly rejected by others, is beyond the shadow of a doubt the Magna Carta against Christological and ecclesiological relativism in this moment of so much confusion.

Pope Francis met not long ago with the Russian Orthodox Patriarch Kirill. It was a great moment of unity, a concrete gesture of desire for closer relations. A theological dialogue with the Orthodox is also necessary. Much is made of the problem of the papacy, but it is linked to the question of the relationship of the Church with states. It could be said that the central figure of the pope, whom many present as exercising a monarchical power that restricts freedom, actually means the defense of the freedom of the Church against the power of states, which are capable of exercising much more pressure on the local episcopates, as history shows. The episcopal conferences would thus become much more subject to manipulation by public opinion and worldly power. What can you say about that?

The meeting between Pope Francis, as the successor of Saint Peter, and the patriarch of the numerically largest Orthodox Church in Russia, on February 12, 2016, at the José Martí International Airport in Havana, represents another step toward the complete institutional reconciliation and sacramental communion of all the local Churches under the guidance of the bishops. I would like to recall here that Pope Eugene IV met as long ago as 1439 with Metropolitan Isidor of Kiev and All Russia, in the Ecumenical Council of Ferrara-Florence and that both celebrated liturgically and signed the Decree of Union *Laetentur coeli*. In that connection, we should note that the unity of Christ's Church can only be brought about in the *communio ecclesiarum*, respecting the legitimate traditions and autonomies of the great and ancient individual Churches, particularly of the patriarchal ones, which, inspired by the civil model, originated in the Christian East on the basis of a relationship between the Mother Church and each regional daughter Church.

How should we give vigor and theological consistency to the dialogue with the Orthodox Churches without resorting to reductive solutions? Respect for the truth is essential, and goodwill is not enough. We will all have to delve deep into the essence of the exercise of the Roman Pontiff's primacy (*CIC*, cann. 331, 333), as it is defined in relation to the college of bishops (*Lumen gentium*, no. 22b), which has nothing to do with a supplementary provision that was supposedly introduced to replace the episcopal structure of the old Church or with the exercise of a monarchical power or any other form of human power. The bishop of Rome, in his personal succession to Peter, exercises, from the truth of divine revelation, his normal, supreme, full, immediate, and universal power, with the jurisdiction characteristic of a government and the Magisterium, in the service of the unity of the Church. He does not displace apostolic testimony or the authority of the various individual bishops or the episcopate as such, but, rather, through his papal power, he strengthens and defends theirs (*Lumen gentium*, no. 27b). The Roman Pontiff carries out the ministry that Christ has entrusted to him subject only to the tutelage of the ecclesial communion, because "in order that the episcopate itself might be one and undivided, He placed Blessed Peter over the other apostles, and instituted in him a permanent and visible source and foundation of unity of faith and communion" (*Lumen gentium*, no. 18).

Peter's office originates in the Gospel: first and foremost, he must safeguard the integrity of the doctrine of the Church ("you are Peter, and on this rock I will build my Church" [Mt 16:18]), a reality that is in itself liberating, dynamic, and life-generating ("Lord, to whom shall we go? You have the words of eternal life" [Jn 6:68]). It is important to say clearly that the free, not the arbitrary, exercise of the pope's power as primate and, specifically, of his infallibility does not in any way restrict the freedom of Christians but, rather, on the contrary, is a guarantee against any temptation to develop a self-referential theology, against any manipulation or falsification of the tenets of faith, and against any attempt at the kind of ideological despoliation that is typical of today's secularized public opinion.

The *munus petrinum* is also one more guarantee protecting the legitimate expectations of the faithful regarding the recognition by modern civil states of their fundamental right to enjoy the freedom of expressing their religion individually and communally or to cooperate with any civil authorities, including public ones, with the common good as their end. In that connection, let me hark back to the international recognition that has always been extended to pontifical diplomacy throughout its centuries-long history. The pope recalls, therefore, that the independence of the Church has to be respected by civil authorities and that the local Churches must remain immune to any form of servility or to yielding to pressure or spurious interests that have their origin in reasons of state.

The fight for *libertas Ecclesiae* has always been a struggle for the liberty of civil society as a whole in its legitimate aspiration to enjoy spheres of independence from the exercise of public power. As the Church defended her freedom from the emperor within a theocracy, there took shape in Europe, little by little, the need to guarantee the autonomy of other actors in civil society, such as guilds, brotherhoods, and all sorts of other civic associations.

How did this dynamic, so important for our current conception of the necessary limits on political power, come into being? It is helpful here to recall the monastic and ascetic movement that, through a great spiritual reform, confronted the new danger of a "feudal secularization" of the Church in the tenth century (see Christopher Dawson, *Religion and the Rise of Western Culture*). Odo of Cluny saw that the chief social evil that had emerged after the overthrow and dismemberment of the Carolingian Empire was the oppression of the poor, which, rooted as it was in the sinful nature of man, could not be countered through recourse only to external means such as the "secular arm". In any case, the fragmentation and anarchy that were endemic to feudal society did not impede, but rather favored, the foundation by Odo of Cluny, Romuald of Ravenna, Abbo of Fleury, Poppo of Stavelot, William of Volpiano, Gerard of Brogne, Bavo, Omer, Bertino, Ghislain, Benigno, Ricardo, of new reformed religious institutions as islands of peace, progress, and spiritual order, without interference from the king or the bishops.

When these reformers came to the Roman Curia in the eleventh and twelfth centuries, among them Hildebrand, who was later known as Gregory VII, they transformed the papacy into the hierarchical center and executive organ of the movement, with the principal objective of affirming the independence and supremacy of spiritual power in the social life of Christianity, in the face of an empire that was weak and incapable of continuing to perform the universal functions of Charlemagne's empire. Emperor Henry IV's ambition to dominate the life of the Church, which theretofore could have been a normal expression of theocratic unity, was then considered an assault on the freedom of the City of God. When the temporal authority erred, it was the obligation of the Church, in the exercise of her complete independence, to call it to order and, if necessary, depose it. The reformist movement, not without profound tensions and rifts, thus gained enough spiritual energy and moral prestige to transform the entire medieval culture and the future of Western Europe.

I would not want to conclude this chapter on what we can hope for from the Church without asking you about the figure of Mary. Lumen gentium (no. 8) avoids an abstract image of Mary by

*presenting her in the context of the Church. If Mary is repre-
sentative of the Church, does this not mean that the Church
herself is a personal Church, that we can address her as if she
were our mother? In addition, is this choice on the part of the
conciliar Fathers not an invitation to all Christians to understand
the importance of a sound Marian devotion? How important is it
to the confession of faith in Jesus and adherence to the Church to
have a veneration of Mary that is more than a mere manifestation
of emotion? More specifically, Your Eminence, is it not precisely
the devotion to Mary that fosters the integration of the emotions
in personal devotion and in a recognition of the truths of our faith?*

Pope Francis, in his simple but exquisitely acute way,
commenting in one of his morning homilies in Santa
Marta on the worldly spirit of curiosity that, at the end of
the day, just generates confusion, made a statement that
wisely summarizes many treatises on Mariology: speaking of whether to consult a supposed clairvoyant who is
receiving messages from the Virgin, it must be made clear
that "the Virgin is Mother. She loves us all. But she is
not a postmistress, there to transmit messages every day.…
These messages distance us from the gospel, from the Holy
Spirit, from peace and wisdom, from the glory of God,
from God's beauty."

The Word of God reveals to us that she is the woman
who, divinely privileged, transmits maternal love to any
disciple of Jesus who wants to receive that filiation in
grace: from Genesis ("I will put enmity between you
and the woman, and between your seed and her seed; he
shall bruise your head, and you shall bruise his heel" [Gen
3:15]) to the Apocalypse ("And a great sign appeared in
heaven, a woman clothed with the sun, with the moon
under her feet, and on her head a crown of twelve stars"
[Rev 12:1]), by way of his first "manifestations" at Cana in

Galilee ("O woman, what have you to do with me? My hour has not yet come" [Jn 2:4]) or in Jerusalem or at Calvary ("When Jesus saw his mother, and the disciple whom he loved standing near, he said to his mother, 'Woman, behold, your son!'" [Jn 19:26]). Jesus wanted the merciful love of his Mother, the Mother who loves us, as the pope recalls, to be present when he performed his first miracle in the sacramental marital context of Cana and when his blood was spilled on the Cross as the price of mankind's redemption.

Saint Joseph, Mary's husband, by divine mandate ("When Joseph woke from sleep, he did as the angel of the Lord commanded him; he took his wife" [Mt 1:24]), faithfully fulfilled his vocation to protect and participate in the upbringing of Jesus and then, after the latter reached the age of twelve, disappeared from the biblical scene, but the Virgin, on the other hand, accompanied her Son throughout his whole public life. The Church, the great teacher, has therefore distinguished between the cult of veneration ("dulia") of all the saints, the "protodulia" of Saint Joseph, and the "hyperdulia", or superveneration, of our Lady. The Virgin's faith grew as her life went on ("B. *Virgo in peregrinatione fidei processit*" [*Lumen gentium*, no. 58]), but faith in her also grew in the personal life of the faithful and of the Church herself over the centuries, to the point of having defined certain truths only recently.

Although the title that the Blessed Paul VI bestowed on her as "Mother of the Church" did not appear in the council (which used other titles, such as *Mater hominum* [*Lumen gentium*, no. 54], *Mater fidelium in ordine gratiae* [*Lumen gentium*, no. 61]), it was the first council in history that "proposed to the Church a doctrinal exposition of Mary's role in the redemptive work of Christ and in the life of the Church" (Saint John Paul II, audience of

December 13, 1995), resituating Mary as the starting point and center of the mystery of salvation and as the personal prefiguration of the Church in the order of faith, of charity, and of the perfect union with Christ (*Typus Ecclesiae*, in the well-known expression of Saint Ambrose). So in referring to the foundations of the Catholic faith, the conciliar documents have emphasized, with respect to the "hierarchy of truths" (*Unitatis redintegratio*, no. 11), that theologians and preachers should especially avoid two risks: on the one hand, that of falsely exaggerating *per excessum*, attributing to the Virgin what is not attributable to her (for example, the Church, despite Mary's privileged position on the work of salvation, does not call her "co-redeemer", because the only Redeemer is Christ and she herself has been redeemed *sublimiore modo*, as *Lumen gentium* [no. 53] says, and serves this redemption wrought exclusively by Christ); and, on the other hand, to deny her *per defectum* the unique privileges that are due her by divine decision (*Lumen gentium*, no. 67)—that is, dogmas such as her Immaculate Conception, her divine maternity, her perpetual virginity, and her Assumption, body and soul, to heavenly glory.

And the private apparitions of the Virgin?

The council does not address the private apparitions of the Virgin, despite the curious phenomenon of the explosion of Marian appearances that have happened recently in the Church for many different reasons; reasons that must be related, in any case, to the diagnosis of today's society that we are discussing here. Such private apparitions, which are not official or binding and add nothing to revealed truth, are taking over more and more space in the media and oblige us as pastors to exercise a delicate and not always effortless discernment, because the *lex orandi* follows the *lex credendi*—that is, we pray what we believe.

Some of these private apparitions are declared to be authentic, making them available to the faithful so that they may better live the revealed truths. The Virgin has done so much good from the Hill of Tepeyac, from the grotto of Lourdes, or from the Cave of Iria, in Fatima! In other cases, decisively and firmly, after a process of serious study and above all accompanied by the prayers of the Church, they are declared false. In that regard, I want to recognize again the Congregation for the Doctrine of the Faith, which in recent centuries has carried out this work, not coldly and bureaucratically, but with an authentic spirituality of service: loving the Holy Father and the Church deeply and intimately, studying with care, patience, and discretion the enormous amount of material that it receives every day, and above all accepting the personal suffering that is always occasioned by an awareness of the sin and misery that hide behind a phenomenon of pseudomysticism.

As happened with Saint Peter when he was in prison and "earnest prayer was made to God by the Church" (Acts 12:5), all Christians but especially we members of the Roman Curia are called to pray for the pope in the difficult decisions that he must make and the pressure, incomprehension, or indiscriminate attacks to which he can be subjected as a result. Saint Catherine of Siena wrote to Urban VI: "I know Your Holiness has a great desire to have helpers who help you" (*Letter* 302).

III

WHAT CAN WE HOPE FOR FROM THE FAMILY?

Let us now take up the subject of the family. Is the family really the hope of society?

The heart of every man and of every woman beats with a desire for fulfillment that can only be met in the communion of life, not in solitude. The story of Genesis, all of it, is especially illustrative of this fact. "The man gave names to all cattle, and to the birds of the air, and to every beast of the field; but for the man there was not found a helper fit for him" (Gen 2:20). The man, in his original solitude, became aware of the difference between himself and the other living beings and, at the same time, of the necessity of a being who would be similar to him. In his self-awareness, he discovered how to be open and await the communion of other people. He discovered, therefore, that he was created "in our [God's] image, after our likeness" (Gen 1:26–27), not only in his humanity but also in his vocation for communion with others.

"Male and female he created them" (Gen 1:27)—that is, twofold in their masculinity and femininity, radically different and fully complementary. In their exact complementarity and in their similitude, the man and the woman saw that they were, each to the other, "helpers" who were "fit" for each other, with whom to bring their lives to fruition (see Gen 2:18, 20). That perfect sexual complementarity constitutes matrimonial love in its two essential properties under natural law: indissolubility and unity (see *CIC*, can. 1056). It is that way because the stability conferred by the properties of "forever" and exclusiveness, as they were desired by God, permits the safekeeping at the same time of the gift of reciprocal personal and exclusive fidelity (*bonum fidei*), the embrace of children, and their education (*bonum prolis*): see *Gaudium et spes*, no. 48. The foundation of that stability, when the union is between two who have been baptized, is the indissoluble union of Christ and his Church, sacramentally represented by that marriage (*bonum sacramenti*): in that case it is understood that it would be impermissible for a Christian to contract a second marriage while the first spouse is still alive, because a bond that has been lawfully created is indissoluble, perpetual. Because of all that, the love that sustains the matrimonial bond, which in a certain way corresponds to the character (*res et sacramentum*) imparted in baptism, in confirmation, and in the sacrament of ordination, must never be reduced to a mere autoreflexive or self-referential sentiment, but should always be seen as a will that, recognizing the great gift that has been received, dedicates itself definitively and with all its strength to the other.

"Be fruitful and multiply" (Gen 1:22). The indissoluble dedication is also fertile, for it carries with it the possibility of communicating itself to others and, therefore, is open to generating a new reality, a child, thereby enlarging the existence of the parents. The child, on the other hand, although he never loses his essential relationship with his own parents, will always be a person in himself with his own subsistence and a singular and unrepeatable vocation for eternity. With these premises, we understand to what extent faith illuminates the greatness that goes with bringing a child into the world: this comes directly from the acts of God. Each of us has been the object of God's thought and love before we were the object of the thought and love of our parents (see Jer 1:5): a child should therefore never be thought of as a "wanted child", as is so in vogue today.

The family, whose principal analogy is the Church, is the social reality that best expresses hope for mankind. Both institutions challenge head-on the individualism that holds sway today. The marriage that is the foundation of every family and enriches the Church, with its invitation to live in an absolutely free unity, expands people's hearts and integrates them in an authentic communion where violence, self-interest, and manipulation have no place. Promising something greater than one's own solitude and inviting its members to love one another freely, it enriches their lives in every respect.

But it appears that today's young people do not assess their future that way. Statistics in the West show an alarming diminution in the number of marriages. Marriage is seen no longer as a promise that opens the way forward in life, but as an option once everything has been resolved. Does that reflect a crisis of hope?

It is not easy today to hold a steady job and find affordable housing, and the accelerated pace of life and the way we spend our free time do not make things any easier. These are just a few of the many external impediments that make it very difficult for young people to get married and raise a family. But I do not believe that this is the key to the real problem. In fact, those difficulties are mitigated by some technical solutions offered by social policies for families. But, even so, we would still be dealing only with symptoms, not with the heart of the matter.

The problem is, if you will allow the expression, that our eyes are ill: yes, I am talking about an illness that affects our vision of what makes life great and beautiful. Our contemporaries are being directly attacked by the virus of the new ideologies, with their attempt to relativize marriage and the family by presenting them as just another option. It is like a pandemic.

The institution of marriage has come to depend on one simple option. It is true that every person who gets married makes a personal choice: specifically, the choice to live faithfully and forever as a couple. This is not a choice about how to deal with sexuality, for one who marries consents to something that happens inside him and carries with it an intrinsic truth: that of the love he has received and been promised. A person who is the object of a great love and feels the call to respond to it knows very well that it is not all there is to marriage or the family. That comes with the experience of loving, and he therefore accepts that call.

Today, however, there is a dangerous redefinition of love based on feelings, which also depicts the family from the perspective of utility and satisfaction, not from the truth that is etched in the intimacy of this experience. Still more surprising is the political use that is being made of this sick ideological vision, fueling from within our main social institutions an authentic social revolution in which everyone is free to decide, according to his whim and will, how to live the sexuality he wants, even though this means denaturalizing the family as the central institution of our society. What is more, this ideology is supported by social repression, even in the form of criminal legislation, of criticizing as a homophobe or stigmatizing as a danger to society anyone who does not accept this "right to choose".

To answer your question: A vision of marriage based on one's own desire and feeling does not offer hope. That is because it does not open the way to anything greater than my own individual plans. I do not understand how we can be so unaware of our own future if in this almost suicidal way we allow our youth to have no higher or more far-reaching horizon than their own feelings.

You used the word "right". Is it not our "right" to have our desires respected and thereby be allowed to act as we want?

Human rights are founded on human nature, not on the desires of individuals. There are rights and obligations only where the authentic dignity of the human being is preserved, because that is the only way for it to realize its fullness.

This is not a matter of denying desires, which are essential to our experience that we have an innate need for infinity; instead, it is a matter of valuing the rationality that those desires carry with them. For example, the desire to live without working, perhaps by using other people's money, should never be a right. If someone does not want to work who is able to do so, he should not have the right to require others to support him, and even less to appropriate to himself what is theirs. It is not a rational desire, precisely because its object is not a good that fulfills life. We all understand this.

The same thing happens in the context of feelings and sex. Someone may say that he has a desire to live not just with one woman but with this other one and that one, too. Because he desires it, he presents it as a need that should be respected by others. This desire should never gain legal recognition, however, because it is not founded on any right that should be recognized as such by society as a whole. Similarly, even if you suppose that the three women agree to this form of cohabitation, their will cannot generate any right because that way of living sexuality, since it does not allow the exclusivity or totality that are elements of love, does not constitute human fulfillment. Responsible citizens, on the other hand, should never yield to the intolerable pressure of the ideology based on the extraordinary thinking that confuses desires with subjective rights and therefore should oppose any such argument, before it is too late, with all the legitimate means that the rule of law affords.

It is true that our society imposes ways of life that make it very hard for families to live their vocation to the full. What should be done about this situation?

Yes, we have to react against a passive acceptance of the different "models of the family" that this Western society, seemingly gone mad, imposes on us. The family is what it is, which is to say, a stable union between a man and a woman that is open to life. It is said that we are living today in a world of technology and science and that we therefore have to adjust our way of life to the model and what it requires. To that, however, we must retort that exterior conditions depend on interior ones, not vice versa.

Let us look at history, the great teacher: the powerful landowners of the southern United States thought in the nineteenth century that the economic model of the Confederacy could not survive without slaves. Economic necessity, they said, dictated their way of life, even if it violated human dignity. But was it a necessity or an abdication? Nor did the need for rapid industrialization of the

Soviet Union during the first half of the twentieth century justify the massive sentences of forced labor or the grueling work routines to which a great part of the population was subjected: this totalitarian Communist regime dismissed the fact that man is the center of the world. This is the wonderful surprise that Christ has communicated to us: because God deeply loves every man and every woman, everything has been created for them, and because they have been marked for glory as the adopted children of God, they are the center of everything. What surprising humanism runs through Holy Scripture!

The new anti-family ideologies, on the other hand, are a new attempt to redefine what is human, based, not on the truth, but on individual feeling and social utility. It is in fact a reinterpretation of pre-Christian paganism, although clearly aimed at social manipulation. There is nothing more controllable than an unintegrated person, with no family ties, with no history, and with no aim in life other than comfort, even if it is low-quality: he is offered *panem et circenses* as in the days of ancient Rome, but in a modern and digital version.

The family has always been the generator of humanity and, therefore, of culture. It is true that the young people of today are marrying less. But, at the same time, we see that in sociological surveys the most highly valued social institution is still the family. It therefore seems as though, at heart, young people feel distrust and nostalgia. How can we address this problem that has settled into the hearts of young people? Does it not motivate us to strengthen the "human fabric" that the family weaves in people's lives?

Yes, it does. We live in cities that do not foster family life. If a man and a woman work long hours outside the house, if they then spend a little time in their hobbies or social life, if in addition they have to satisfy their family obligations ... anybody can understand that we are dealing with serious conditions that get in the way of a healthy family life. I do not believe, however, that we should consider these conditions a fixed standard by which we value what the family can offer, as though the family were the variable and these circumstances were the fixed unknown.

Attempts to reconcile the schedules with each other are, in this sense, very positive: they are in themselves a good beginning, but they are insufficient and certainly no panacea. In addition, we must consider that the concept of reconciliation presupposes the opposition of two realities as though they were antithetical to each other: work and family. If we look at Holy Scripture, these two realities have a harmonious relationship in God's plan: Adam and Eve are told to work the land and multiply as a condition of their fulfillment. We, for our part, should rediscover this original covenant between work and family, because they make demands on each other. We must remind spouses that the path to their happiness runs through reliving this original covenant in their own marriage, patiently and generously weaving a harmonious relationship between their family and their work. So many of a couple's joint undertakings have failed, so many children have had their education neglected, because of this problem! Excessive dedication to work, which makes work incompatible with inescapable family obligations, has generated so much dissatisfaction!

Your question brings up a major issue: marriages today are very alone in facing the great task that they have before them. We of the Church, as well as society, are called to accompany them wisely with a family ministry and a responsible family policy that are able to generate hope, especially in young people.

The family is the first environment in which the Church and the world meet. Exactly that can be seen very clearly in the framework of the two most recent synods on the family, which have again brought to our attention the family as a privileged place of dialogue with the modern world. But there has been a new development since the time of the Second Vatican Council. Then the great difficulty was the crisis of the middle-class family. Today, on the other hand, we speak of a crisis in family structure as such. What is in crisis today is the sense of the very difference in sexuality, emptying it of meaning when it comes to talking about "family models". How should we confront this new crisis? Can we still hope for something from the family in this context?

Today's challenges are enormous. The systematic attacks that were made in the twentieth century against everything that sustains man in his humanity have caused the rapid secularization of many countries with a deep Christian tradition. At the origin of this apostasy, which in some places is pervasive, lies the denaturalization of faith, reducing the Christian religion to a collection of values, of ideas, and of social activities that in the end interest no one. When we went in this direction, we cut our umbilical cord to the source, blocking true communication with Jesus Christ, the only Savior of man, thereby making it impossible to give meaning to basic institutions like the sacrament of marriage.

Marriage is not just a decision to live with another person but, rather, the firm resolution to be "one flesh" in the context of the relationship of Jesus Christ with his spouse the Church: "For this reason a man shall leave his father and mother and be joined to his wife, and the two shall become one flesh" (Mk 10:78). The conjugal union fully enters the center of the spousal love of Christ for the Church and her potential of love, in which Christian spouses share on the day of their marriage. It follows that the purpose of marriage is not only natural but also supernatural: the sanctification of the spouses and of life, to be able thereby to reach full communion with God (see *Lumen gentium*, no. 11). This sacrament attains its full depth when it is seen from the perspective of the union between Christ the husband with his wife the Church: by divine will, the man and the woman are called to be *one single beloved*, thereby originating and giving life to the entire family.

Christian doctrine reminds us of this essential point: the intimate union of two Christian spouses is not based on the feelings they may experience or on their will to stay together. It is founded on the gift that the Lord has given them as the first consequence of the sacrament, to be able to live bonded forever in marriage. This bond, which should be recognized by the spouses as such, will be the great adventure of their lives. It will also be their great reason for hope, because it is a firm rock on which they will be able to build the entire edifice of their future existence and from which they will be able to enjoy beautiful moments and also successfully weather their difficult moments and storms.

To answer your question more specifically, of course we can place our hope in the family! It is in the family that the greatness and magnanimity of the divine plan is realized, which has made the family the road to salvation. The family is fulfillment, the sacred space in which we can be with God: as Mount Horeb was to Moses, it is a place where we should reverently take off our shoes from our feet (see Ex 3:5), because God speaks to us there. It is also a place that today's Church should take as her favored path. I repeat: we cannot remain indifferent to the attempt to relativize marriage and the family. They are not "just another option".

We are also facing an educational challenge of the first order: we will have to give our children and youth a better education, accompany them better with our witness to life so that, as they progress in maturity, they are prepared for an indissoluble marriage, the only one that will make them truly happy. We will have to warn them against sex as a mere occasion for pleasure. We will have to explain better to them that God has cherished sexual pleasure, considering it a noble sign of a personal truth and an instrument for tasting the joy of interpersonal communion. We will have to tell them, in all truth, that only sex between two spouses, not sporadic sexual relations, permits the communication of the Word in the soul of the beloved. We will have to invite them to seek human fulfillment in living their love as spouses or as consecrated to the Lord as forms of participating in God's love.

Internal preparation for marriage, whether remote, near at hand, or immediate, belongs at the heart of Christian education. Educating our children is not just about giving them technical studies or learning foreign languages; it is also about helping them overcome a way of living sexuality that reduces it to an experiment to be enjoyed. Teaching them well means helping them recognize progressively in sex that personal and integral dimension which unites all the fundamental elements of human existence: the individual, community, human sociability, responsibility, generation.

Hope for the family is a challenge and a task. No one can guarantee that this family which has been constituted on your son's or your daughter's wedding day will attain fulfillment. That is an undertaking not only of the spouses, of their families, or of the friends who accompany them on that day: the Church herself, Christ's spouse, is called to accompany marriages and to foster families capable of creating a familial spirit in their environments and

social surroundings. I believe priests should not only better organize the prematrimonial counseling in their parishes, they should dedicate more time to the families they
know, attending to them pastorally and sacramentally and
overseeing their education more enthusiastically and with
greater engagement.

*Pope Francis has warned against the danger of an "ideological
colonization" of the family. What he is talking about is precisely
that ideology which destroys the individual, because it destroys his
family ties. We have talked a lot here about ideology, but what is
ideology as such? Karl Marx defined it as "the means of attaining
an undeclared goal". Are there glimpses of "undeclared goals" in
the ideological attack against the family?*

Gender ideology, which is behind this attack on the family, may serve as a good example for understanding what
an ideology is. Basically it is a complete conception of the
person, taking as its starting point a concatenation of principles for a particular logical structure that does not respect
the reality of things and that ultimately denies the Creator
and man's condition of having been created.

Ideologies can be interconnected. So, for example,
atheism clothes itself in a vague evolutionism, as if it were
a simple bio-scientific fact. This evolutionism ultimately
turns into an ideological tool for justifying atheism. What
is undeclared in this ideology? Marx and many later ideo-
logues made their stand on the principle of man's autosal-
vation: man creates and recreates himself continuously and
therefore becomes his own and only possible redeemer. It
is common in this kind of thinking to see man as a demiurge of himself and of the things that surround him, as a
kind of colonizer of chaotic matter.

With these principles, it is understood that there may be an ideological construction that affirms that man's identity does not depend on nature, with a body that is limited to a masculine or feminine sexuality. This ideology makes use of medical advances to use the body as an area of experimentation, viewing a change in sex as a simply biological operation.

There is an evident dualism behind all this: the body loses its significance vis-à-vis its own identity. It is self-made on the basis of its own feelings or desires, not on the basis of its being. That is what I mean when I say that the person becomes a demiurge that acts according to its own freedom and its own desires, simply giving them expression in any material thing, including the body. Pope Francis has unmasked this pretension, pointing out that it is a genuine "ideological colonization", in which "they take, they actually take the need of a people to seize an opportunity to enter and grow strong—through the children", he said, during his return flight from the Philippines to Rome on January 19, 2015, giving as an example a government employee who was given a loan for the construction of schools for the poor on the condition that gender ideology be included in the study plan. "Every threat to the family is a threat to society itself", the pontiff had said earlier (January 16, 2015) in his visit.

What is undeclared in this totalitarian pretension? An idol: we have made an idol of our own liberty, of our own wish, proposing to be, ourselves, those who determine what is good and bad. Was this not the substance of the first temptation of Adam and Eve? Is it possible to build a society without respecting the fundamental difference between a man and a woman?

In this sometimes desolate landscape, I also see many reasons for hope. In a speech to which we will frequently return, which Saint John Paul II gave on October 10, 1980, in the "Conference on Evangelization and Atheism", we find many clarifying words *in merito*: this pontiff affirmed that modern man, resisting the repeated assaults of pragmatic, neopositivist, psychoanalytic, existentialist, Marxist, structuralist, Nietzschean atheism, ... has actually achieved the opposite effect—that is, the resurgence of a religious reawakening.

Now we understand better that "man is the path of the Church", that same man who today has been wounded and abused by ideologies, robbed of his hopes, as in the parable of the good Samaritan mentioned above: the Church addresses herself to precisely this man, to help him discover his humanity and regenerate his hope.

John Paul II himself reformulated this phrase in his Letter to Families, in affirming that "the family is the way of the Church." That is how the Holy Father proclaimed it. What does this mean?

Family is not reducible to a mere sociological reality, conditioned by certain political or economic situations. Nor is it born of society. It is born of the divine design itself as a social reality capable of giving form to society. Its foundation is the mutual and reciprocal love between one man and one woman, which is the image of divine love and therefore a love open to life. When one understands that this love comes from God, is realized in God, and binds us to God, he understands why the family is the way of the Church. In the family we discover that the life of every new man comes directly from love, and this discovery is also an ecclesial itinerary: we recognize this path in the gifts of conjugal love and new life.

We must therefore make every effort to vindicate and support parents because of their decisive role. They are "ministers of creation", at the service of all of it and of the creatures most prized by God, his children. It is a true service to life, because in God's plan they are his collaborators, recreating what he has made. In fact, the child that they have engendered is not their property or even an object that is at their disposal: they have received him as a gift that God has entrusted to them.

It is very important to understand that this proposition is not just one more ideology, or even an anti-ideology, but rather it is a non-ideology, a liberation from all ideologies. An ideology, as we have seen, is a logical structure at the service of a man whose purpose is to dominate others. Totalitarianisms, which have fragmentation, extreme individualism, as their very close "twin", are the supreme example of it. Let us not forget that we live in what Benedict XVI has repeatedly denounced as the "dictatorship of relativism". Because in every totalitarianism one finite being becomes absolute, and thus in the name of a false freedom, through arbitrariness and violence, he wounds the two most sacred forms of freedom: that of conscience and that of religion. To achieve that, ideologies always seek to transform the communion among persons into an undifferentiated mass.

The Church, however, is a communion based on the reality that follows the path of that communion of individuals which is the family. The Church will never take the path of the "mass". When, for example, the pope addresses young people in one of his many encounters with them, even with millions of people, he does not address them *en masse*. They constitute a living people of specific individuals, every one of them a mystery in the great mystery of love that is God: those millions of faithful gathered there are a communion of persons who, brought together by the Other, have found each other. In fact, every one of them is there because he has earlier found Jesus Christ. They may not understand fully, because they speak many very different languages, but there is in them a profound comprehension of the heart, called communion, that unites them. They do not meet with the pope as an individual but as the Vicar of Christ. The pope speaks, not of himself, but of Jesus Christ. The pope, as Francis recalls again and again, never occupies the place that belongs exclusively to God, and therefore the pope wants to be treated that way: this is the great difference between him and a dictator who, presenting himself as the center and culmination of social life, fosters the cult of his own personality.

We Christians flee from the personality cult. We reject it as an idolatrous temptation. For that reason we are always careful not to focus on the man, even if he is the pope: we cannot applaud him and at the same time ignore his message about Jesus Christ. We cannot consider the pope as a global personality of the first order and not at the same time receive his Petrine ministry. We cannot acclaim the pope when he speaks to us of mercy and not commit ourselves, exigently, to loving our neighbor. We cannot praise him when he speaks against corruption and then not come to terms, every one of us, with our own need for conversion.

Let us return to the family. Can it be said that the family is an "ideal"? I remember in that connection the accusation that the novelist Bernanos puts in the mouth of the countess in his famous Diary of a Country Priest. *The countess is living in an unsustainable situation in her family: her husband is deceiving her with her daughter's teacher, and her daughter is aware of it, besides. In her dialogue with the priest regarding the advice and warnings he gives her, she replies: "You don't know what I have suffered. You don't know anything about life. . . . Oh, you priests have a naïve and absurd idea of family life." In the course of the conversation, however, the priest reveals to the countess what the reason for her sadness and despondency is, which she recognizes in the end: "I have willfully sinned against hope." The countess did not know how to find the gift she had received in her family, and she despaired over her inability to do so. We are told we should address reality, so what is real in the family? Do we not run the risk of hoping for too little from the family, of conceiving of the family as only a beautiful "ideal"? Or is the countess right and our vision of the family is naïve and absurd?*

The categories of the ideal and the real go back very far in time, specifically to the philosophical proposition of Plato. In their current form, however, they originate in the metaphysical dualism of Descartes' philosophy and in idealist and materialist dualism. Idealism holds that reality is only an epiphenomenon of the ideal world, elaborated by the mind. Materialists hold, for their part, that reality is matter and the rest is just a construct of the human brain, aimed at satisfying its own interests.

For us, these dualisms have no validity at all. God is always more real than his creation, and his creatures receive their measure as a gift from him, for he realized his idea in the creation. All of creation reflects the *Logos* of God, so marriage is not an "ideal" that men have imagined. An ideal is the reflection of my desire, like the child who wants to be an astronaut or a soccer star ... even though only a tiny minority achieve their dream. An ideal, in fact, is usually unattainable: it would be ideal if all the world's countries were to collaborate with each other to end, once and for all, the scourge of hunger, but the reality is otherwise, on account of a thousand and one competing interests. To be able to survive this state of continuous disappointment, we usually adapt our ideals to what really happens: "Since I won't be able to get what I wanted", I say to myself, "I'll settle for expecting something less than what I had dreamed of."

Marriage, however, is not an ideal or a human idea, but a reality given by God. Remember that the gospel does not consist of new ideas, either; instead, its true originality lies in Christ himself, who "gives flesh and blood to concepts" (Benedict XVI, *Deus caritas est*, no. 12). It is he who, in an unprecedented form, has created man and woman for love, both of them open to a relationship and fecundity: this is not an idea but a reality and, at the same time, a promise of fulfillment. God's way of loving is the measure of human love, for God does not ask the impossible.

A couple's relationship, conceived as a mere ideal, is inevitably doomed to failure. If in prayerful dialogue with God the Father, however, both members of the couple enter into Jesus' act of self-offering in the Eucharist and his dynamic of dedication through love and, thereby, with humility and great generosity come forth from themselves in their dedication to the other, they will attain the maturity that is characteristic of conjugal love, which in addition embraces all their potential. By seeing their relationship with the eyes of Christ, they discover that doing so heals and transforms them.

There are those who say: "Man is not capable of keeping the promise of fulfillment that he has received or of meeting the requirements of marriage or God's commandments." But that is false. God can oblige us to love, because first he has loved us and, in addition, he has promised us that his grace will sustain us. Anyone who understands marriage as nothing more than the social act of the wedding and the legal consequences that flow from it will certainly see his love wither. But not for lack of grace: for lack of the humility necessary to ask God for that grace. The couple must therefore pray constantly for perseverance.

Pastors must repeatedly invite families to join together in the celebration of the Eucharist and to make their confession frequently, to foster in them the ability to ask for forgiveness, without which it will be impossible to face the demands of family life. It is necessary to encourage in every diocese those lay spiritual movements such as Father Caffarel's Teams of Our Lady, which encourage family nuclei where God, in a perfectly normal way, is one of the family, a domestic Church.

How does God accompany spouses?

The conjugal link is not just something to achieve, it is above all a great gift received from God in order to be able to turn those first feelings, which are beautiful even if superficial, into a mature, purified love. It is thereby possible to address marriage as a lifelong task. This union begins with a divine act ("What therefore God has joined together", Mt 19:6), which prompts human action in turn.

No marriage is trouble-free. We suffer because of our finite reality, the limits of our human nature that stem from original sin. That is the reality. We should understand it and accept it from the outset. We should be fully conscious of it, if we want to overcome these problems with the Spirit of Christ. We make a grave mistake, however, if we justify ourselves, because it does no good to offer excuses for our discouragement, our miseries, our failures of fidelity in conjugal life.

Our premarital counseling is often a complete failure because it is founded on mistaken premises: if you explain to the couple no more than the possible dangers that they will have to confront when they are married, you will not be able to explain very well how with their own efforts, capabilities, and qualities they will not be able to succeed in remaining faithful in their love. You have to explain to them clearly that their desire to form a family is not, by itself, enough. You have to bring them face to face with reality and tell them bluntly that many have failed and that, moreover, the reason for their failure has most often been a lack of understanding that love is a gift of God that must be lived generously and cared for every day as the most delicate gift we will ever hold in our hands. Without deceiving them in any way, you have to tell them clearly that today, a family that does not pray stays together with difficulty.

The desire to form a family can lead people to want to build one that answers their emotional needs and, in fact, to construct a personalized "family model", in which they feel comfortable but which does not respect the reality of the members of the family or the role that God must necessarily play in it. That is the reason for so many failures, unfortunately.

So how do we confront tragedy in a marriage? Every marriage is a world of its own, certainly. Do we act case by case? The way Christ behaves is very illustrative, because when he is questioned by the Pharisees about when a divorce may be granted, he answers categorically with a reference to God's original plan: it was a cultural matter in which every case required illumination by the same light. Whereas when he speaks personally with the Samaritan woman, he addresses the question little by little until he reaches the source of the woman's dissatisfaction. In what way can the difference between a cultural answer and a personal answer help to deal with "special cases" and "irregular situations"?

There is something in the marriage that does not fail: living together may fail, or human expectations may fail, but what never fails in it is God's action, because the strength of his action is there *ex opere operato*. God does not fail in his sacramental grace. In arguments, even in arguments between ecclesiastics, we may overlook the distinction between the marriage in itself—which is a natural reality and a sacrament between two baptized persons—and our will to obey God's commandments or not.

Spouses could certainly commit a sin against marital chastity, but this does not mean that the sacrament disappears or is eliminated. These same spouses could even stop living together and be joined with another person, but the sacrament, with the indissoluble bond that comes with it, continues to endure as a demand, as an anchor that can be dropped in the water in the middle of a storm: the sacrament as such does not fail.

What can the Church do to deal with situations of marital difficulty?

The Church's task is always threefold: to spread the unabridged word of God (*martyria*), to celebrate the sacraments faithfully (*leiturgia*), and to serve charity with dedication, not as mere social service, but as an act of loving one's neighbor organically and wholly (*diakonia*). What is essential, then, is that the Church remain faithful to herself and not stop offering the help that God has given us to attain eternal life. This is what people truly hope: not that we justify them, but that we help them live their vocation.

The Church's love remains true. We therefore have to take as our premise that she will never have the authority to dispense with the divine commandments, in the name of a supposedly compassionate and loving vision, in situations that do not conform to the Word of God.

She cannot, for example, grant a second marriage while a first spouse of a sacramental marriage, consummated or unconsummated, is still alive. In certain difficult family situations, the Church can allow an interruption of marital life together, but she cannot break the sacramental bond. The separation of spouses can be an acceptable solution for extreme situations, but what the Church can never do is contradict the divine Word of which she is the mediator.

In the case of a serious difficulty in marital life, the Church should accompany the couple and offer God's mercy again and again, particularly through the sacrament of reconciliation: it is a duty that she discharges person to person, you to you. The Church must recall her message of salvation founded in God's fidelity to his promise: because God is faithful to us, spouses are called to be faithful to their sacramental promise. That is the message that "in season and out of season" (see 2 Tim 4:2) we must keep on preaching.

This message is not an unbearable cross or yoke: it is good news for spouses, reminding them of the greatness and nobility of their vocation. In addition, when it is faithfully transmitted, it confers grace, because the Church, when she transmits the gospel in its entirety, transmits a word that communicates the Spirit.

We are seeing a dramatic decrease in the birthrate in our society. Families are afraid to have children. Why? We hear about economic difficulties or sociological difficulties (social pressure). Are these the obstacles? Would there not be at bottom a reason more deeply rooted in people's hearts, a lack of hope, which keeps them from opening themselves to the gift of fertility? What hope does a large family offer us? Vatican II had spoken of a responsible, generous parenthood. It frequently seems as though we have forgotten the adjective "generous" and kept only "responsible". What can we learn from families to whom the Lord has granted the gift and the task of having many children?

A child is always, under all circumstances, a gift from above. Having been created in the image and likeness of God, every person has been constituted in his self-awareness and self-determination as a *partner* of God and, therefore, contains his mystery within him. A child, therefore, is never a simple human undertaking or the product of a calculation of interests, and although he may have been engendered by his parents in that way, God will have previously conferred on him the sublime dignity of being his child.

The concept of "responsible parenthood" of which the council spoke and which later is taken up in the encyclical *Humanae vitae* does not refer mainly to the circumstances in which to have children or to the consequences, but to the responsibility, greatness, and truth that begetting a person involves: one can welcome the child as a true gift only if he welcomes him through the gift of himself and communicates that to him throughout his life. It is a matter, then, of responding to the gift of God, welcoming the child as such.

This concept has been very badly misinterpreted, however. The adjective "responsible" has been extended to the consequences of having children, thereby projecting expectations or one's own ideas about how the child should be, his education, the effects on the family's resources or situation, even social situation. Based on catastrophic predictions that have never been borne out, rooted in neo-Malthusianism (for example, Paul Ehrlich, *The Population Bomb*), some international organizations have recently exacerbated the problem, proposing a "responsible parenthood" that implies reducing the birthrate, by whatever means, for a better distribution and optimal use of resources.

In that regard, we must clearly denounce as having no scientific basis the claim that the alleged current population explosion has caused global economic impoverishment: if two thousand years ago the world had an estimated two hundred million inhabitants, and it took fifteen centuries to double that population, in the last two centuries the world population has multiplied by six, surpassing six billion inhabitants, while real GDP worldwide has multiplied by fifty. It is no surprise, then, that the anti-birth theories based on the myth of population's geometric progression while the means of subsistence have grown only in arithmetic progression (Thomas Robert Malthus, *An Essay on the Principle of Population*), should be more and more discredited among the scientific community, which now leans more and more to the conclusion that people, when they are seen clearly, unclouded by erroneous ideological distortions (Friedrich Hayek, *The Fatal Conceit*), end up resolving the problems themselves thanks to human creativity.

Anti-birth policies are nothing but another ideological proposal that hides the unmentionable: the attempt to maintain, unfairly, the privileged status of a few, at the expense of blocking access to wealth by broad layers of the population. Actually, as we have just explained, we know that hunger in the world is not at all the consequence of overpopulation and that abortion does nothing to contain population growth, serving only to satisfy our hedonism.

How does true Christian anthropology take shape in the reality of the average family? Do we need better studies to understand the virtue of procreation? Obviously not. Generosity lives even better in simplicity, and I can assure you that many of the parents of our large families of the past had several doctorates in humanity. The generation of a child is an act that is born of the mature personal love of spouses who dedicate themselves totally one to the other with their bodies and with all their being. The sexual act, as the fruit of love, is a true gift of themselves that makes possible another great gift, the child. The body is thus, not just an instrument of pleasure, but a servant of fatherhood and motherhood.

It is therefore for the parents themselves to weigh responsibly whether this is the right moment to welcome a new child into the family. True, in making that evaluation, material, psychological, logistical, educational, and health conditions will also enter into the decision. But these can never be a whole that is closed and given, a simple reckoning of probabilities, but rather is a factor to be added as one part of what is more important to consider, which is what every new child brings into the family. This always generates a new relationship and a new hope among his family. Any family is evidence of this, but especially those that have a child with a serious physical or psychological handicap. In spite of all the difficulties and inconveniences, how much joy, tenderness, and humanity does such a child with Down syndrome bring to his parents and siblings! If they are aware of the gift they have received, they receive a new motivation to address any adversity. I do not doubt that yes, material conditions are important. But what is more important is hope, and children are a source of hope; when we give priority to our calculations and precautions over the gift, we lose that hope.

And large families?

Large families are an expression of the superabundance of love. They are a great yes to life. Several children are a great gift not only for their parents but also for the Church and all of society. *Lumen gentium* (no. 11) speaks of Christian parents as those who in a certain way bestow their children on the Church.

In that connection, I have never understood how Western countries, with negative rates of population growth and ever-increasing rates of life expectancy, do not recognize and sustain the will of those few who, very generously, are inclined to form a large family. On the contrary, those who should be the object of our admiration and respect are irrationally treated with negative mockery or discriminated against with unfair indirect taxes, when they should be favored with special social policies, because even from the point of view of self-interest, those children are our future, and it is they who will support the elderly of tomorrow with their economic contribution.

I should make it clear, so as to avoid being misinterpreted, that it would be superficial to conclude that marriage is there to bring to society well-educated human elements, as a function of its growth and that of the Church. The Magisterium, on the contrary, has always taught that it is not a matter of a simple question of social utility: children are a good in themselves, and they make their parents better, expanding their heart, strengthening their union, and generating in them a new fulfillment, precisely because they become the object of their concern and attention. Children are, for their parents, their teachers in generosity. A large family is a great school of generosity!

There is a noticeable difficulty regarding the reception of Paul VI's encyclical Humanae vitae. *The recent Synod on the Family has certainly confirmed its doctrine. But the stir in the media that it caused shows us that acceptance of this encyclical continues to be problematic. On the other hand, we are witnesses to the surprising vitality of families that embrace the teachings of* Humanae vitae. *Isn't this observation in itself a message and a verification?*

The encyclical *Humanae vitae* had many difficulties in its reception, as much for its underlying anthropology—especially regarding its proposal on the experience of love and sexuality—as for its clarification of the intrinsic morality of the methods of birth control. The indiscriminate attacks to which it was subject from the outset caused it to be marginalized and forgotten, despite its richness in inventively and prophetically posing the reality of love, of marriage, and of the beauty of married life.

Today, almost fifty years later, we see much more clearly that Pope Paul VI was right in everything that at the time he had the courage to make clear. Ahead of his time, this humanist pope had the courage to offer this document to the Church and to society, denouncing with an accurate analysis what ended up happening. Are we not, indeed, witnessing a pandemic of divorce? Have we not, just as unmistakably, turned sex into a trivial reality devoid of feeling? And is it not as patently clear today that Western societies, having radically separated the unitive function from that of procreation, have a true problem in their birthrate? The situation is one of authentic demographic involution that carries grave consequences, considered both synchronically and diachronically, if we examine the present moment and the foreseeable possibilities for the near future.

But the problem, I repeat, is not only demographic but rather, above all, one of meaning: I mean the question of the identity and vitality of marriage. Perhaps five decades ago it was not so evident, since the institution of the family was still strong: in fact, it was not yet foreseen that there could be so many broken marriages in our own families, with so many children who could not enjoy a father and a mother living under the same roof or so many adolescents initiating themselves at a young age in a life of frivolous sex. Yes, we are much more able today to grasp the negative impact of a mistaken conception of sex, valued only for the gratification it brings and not for the gift that it makes possible. We understand better today the perverse effects of artificial birth control, as a simple means toward the worry-free enjoyment of sex, without wanting to see the consequences for physical, psychological, and spiritual health.

Moral problems demand moral solutions. We must humanize sexuality, which is at the service of the personal union of spouses, making it possible for each to be a gift to the other and not only a means for satisfying their desire. We must explain to new spouses the goodness, for example, of natural methods that, based on abstinence from sexual contact during the fertile days, foster dialogue, mutual respect, and understanding in the couple.

The pansexual culture described here poses a challenge to the Church and to all men of goodwill: we must explain the role sex plays in human fulfillment. We cannot go on reducing sexuality to a mere means of self-centered pleasure because the "traditional" idea of marriage is no longer in play, and even less so "bourgeois" marriage. We Christians are not fundamentalists who fight for an obsolete family model, but we are aware of the fact that in reality what is at stake is the truth of love, the feeling of sexuality, the greatness of marriage, the fulfillment of man.

Paul VI, in the service of truth, wanted to teach the conditions that make true love possible between a man and a woman. "The truth will make you free": perhaps this sentence of Christ is the key to understanding the problem of sexuality that has been posed in our lives. The Church, by reminding us of the divine revelation about love and marriage, does no more than teach the only way to live sexuality humanely: all the other ways, in contrast, are frauds that just lead to our progressive dehumanization.

In light of what happened in the case of *Humanae vitae*, I believe that today we must reflect more deeply and avoid future misunderstandings: we should begin at the beginning and thoroughly explore every aspect of it. We should start with the essence of married life and not from the other end, as the media and public opinion do. During the last four decades, these have not stopped pointing to the Church as a puritan and repressive institution on the subject of sex. Caricaturing her as a group of conservative wet blankets, some see her also as an opportunity to put a brake on the preaching of the gospel. It may be that, unintentionally, they have pointed the way for us: the key to humanizing sexuality lies in leading people back to the heart of the gospel.

The Church, accompanied by him who is the Way, the Truth, and the Life (see Jn 14:6), proposes a demanding path because she believes in people and in their ability to reach fulfillment. Her Magisterium, illuminated by revelation, teaches that marriage contains a hierarchy of truths, an internal order of elements: not in the sense that some things are less important than others and therefore dispensable, but in the sense that some of them cause the others. Only if we understand this order is it possible for us to understand, for example, that the Church rejects contraceptive methods because they obstruct spouses' gift of yes. If we turn that rejection into the center of the debate, however, we all end up forgetting that what is truly fundamental is the gift that the spouses receive in the marriage itself, which in turn enables them to live their sexuality as a reciprocal gift that can be an example to others.

At the dawn of Christianity, an indissoluble marriage was a hall-mark of this new way. Neither the Roman nor the Jewish world held the union of two spouses to be indissoluble. Lord Jesus' words in Matthew 19 and later Paul's words in 1 Corinthians 7 and in Ephesians 5 were interpreted as a countercultural novelty. They would not have imposed this requirement on the Christian faithful if they had not understood that it was not a "burden" but the hope of living a greater life, the possibility of opening themselves to an unfailing fidelity. Can the Church change this today? Can she do so in the name of a so-called "development of dogma"?

Nihil novum sub sole! At its beginning, Christianity spread in a culture that freely accepted divorce, especially in the case of a man divorcing his wife. Contrary to this cultural environment, the Church remained faithful to the word of Jesus, to the point of radically transforming society by proclaiming a great hope: with Jesus, it is possible for love to endure for a lifetime and to be renewed amid any difficulties, unshaken by every affront. The Church of the Fathers, in obedience to the gospel, rejected divorce and a second marriage: on this point, the testimony of the Fathers is unequivocal.

Later, in some areas, especially because of the growing interdependence between the Church and the state, in cases even of outright and undue interference, they reached certain compromises. In the East, for example, after the separation of those ecclesial communities from the *Cathedra Petri*, an increasingly liberal praxis or "right of consuetudinary origin" was accepted, under which—after a period of penitence—a second marriage was allowed, even in the case of a valid first marriage and with the first spouse still living, and participation in Communion, as a life preserver that enabled "salvation", was allowed at the same time. As a result, the Orthodox Churches, by the principle of *oikonomia* or pastoral condescension (called the "pastoral approach of tolerance, clemency, and indulgence") went on to justify a multitude of reasons for divorce. Considering the words of Jesus concerning the indissolubility of marriage, I do not see how this practice can be derived from the will of God.

In the West, the Gregorian Reform opposed this liberalizing tendency and asserted the original interpretation of Scripture and of the Fathers. Applying the same principle, the Catholic Church defended the absolute indissolubility of marriage, both consummated and unconsummated, even at the cost of great sacrifice and suffering.

One example of that is the schism of the Church of England, separated from Peter's successor in dramatic circumstances. The causes of the separation were not doctrinal differences but the refusal of Pope Clement VII to yield to the pressure of King Henry VIII for dissolution of his valid marriage with Catherine of Aragon. Saint Thomas More, from prison, expressed the problem well in one of his letters to his daughter Margaret: "His grace has strengthened me until now and made me content to lose goods, land, and life as well, rather than to swear against my conscience."

The Council of Trent confirmed the doctrine of the indissolubility of sacramental marriage and explained that this corresponded to the teaching of the Gospel (see DH 1807). It did so, not abstractly, but in response to a concrete case that Luther had presented: the case of one who had been wrongfully abandoned by his spouse. The Council of Trent thus analyzed a specific case, the most extreme one, and concluded that even in this eventuality, in which everything pointed toward not trusting to love, Christian hope still continued to prevail. This council taught, therefore, that a love that embraces a lifetime is possible.

Recently, on the occasion of the latest Synod on the Family, it has again been argued that the Church in fact tolerated the Eastern praxis, but this is not exactly consistent with historical truth: the experts in canon law repeatedly characterized this practice as abusive, and there are testimonies by groups of Orthodox Christians who, when they converted to Catholicism, had to sign a confession of faith with express reference to the impossibility of a second or third marriage. The Second Vatican Council, for its part, in the Pastoral Constitution *Gaudium et spes* on the Church in the Modern World, recorded yet again the theological and spiritual doctrine that underlies the indissolubility of marriage (see *Gaudium et spes*, nos. 48 and 50).

There followed the Familiaris consortio *of John Paul II, which specifically addressed this thorny issue of divorce and civil remarriage . . .*

That is right. The text of the apostolic exhortation *Familiaris consortio,* published by John Paul II on November 22, 1981, and fundamental even today, expressly confirmed the dogmatic teaching of the Church on marriage. But also, from the pastoral point of view, this document manifested a special concern and sympathy for the faithful who have contracted a new civil union although still married in a previous valid ecclesiastical marriage.

In that respect, this apostolic exhortation in number 84 ("Divorced Persons Who Have Remarried") makes the following fundamental affirmations:

1. Pastors who have souls in their care are obligated by the love of truth to "exercise careful discernment of situations": they should not judge everything and everyone in the same way.

2. Pastors and communities are obligated to help, with solicitous charity, the divorced faithful who have remarried civilly: the criterion should be their integration in the Church, for they, too, are her members, have the right to pastoral attention, and should participate in her life.

3. It is not possible, however, to grant them access to the Eucharist, for two reasons: "their state and condition of life objectively contradict that union of love between Christ and the Church which is signified and effected by the Eucharist", and "if these people were admitted to the Eucharist, the faithful would be led into error and confusion regarding the Church's teaching about the indissolubility of marriage." In addition, a reconciliation through the sacrament of penance, which would open the way to Eucharistic Communion, would only be possible in the event of repentance regarding what has happened and a readiness to undertake "a way of life that is no longer in contradiction to the indissolubility of marriage". This means, in practice, that when there are serious reasons that the new union cannot be interrupted, such as those relating to the childrens' upbringing, the man and woman who want to receive the Eucharist would be bound to live in complete continence.

4. Pastors are expressly prohibited, for theological-sacramental reasons and not merely legal ones, from performing "ceremonies of any kind" for divorced people who remarry while the first marriage continues to be valid.

The Synod on the Family held in 2015 has explored this perspective further. In the months leading up to the synod, a solution to the problem of divorced people who have been remarried civilly was proposed that came close to that of the Orthodox Churches, to which I referred before. The proposal was to begin a new penitential praxis based on the principle of God's infinite mercy, applied to certain situations, case by case, through the *discretio* or spiritual discernment of pastors.

During the work of the synod, however, there again was insistence that, given the intimate nature of the sacraments and the character of the indissolubility of marriage as divine law, it is not possible to admit to the Eucharist divorced people who have remarried civilly.

In that connection, we must, on the one hand, not forget that the whole sacramental order is a work of divine sanctity, justice, and mercy. The last of these, as it appears in the Word of God, should never be understood as a "dispensation" from the commandments of God and the Church or as a "justification" for suspending and invalidating them: "Go, and do not sin again" (Jn 8:13), Jesus said to the adulteress after he had treated her with great mercy. In fact, God in his infinite mercy grants the strength of grace to fulfill his commandments completely and thereby reinstill in us, after the Fall, his perfect image as the Heavenly Father. Saint Thomas, moreover, as I recalled in my earlier work *The Hope of the Family*, affirmed that mercy is precisely the fulfillment of justice, for in it God justifies and renews the creation of man (see *Summa Theologica* I, q. 21, a. 3).

On the other hand, because the indissolubility of sacramental marriage is a norm of divine law, an irregular situation of such a nature should be met by the Church with a reaffirmation of that indissolubility to the faithful; an insistence on the need for them to be in communion with God and in his way of sanctification as elaborated in *Familiaris consortio* (no. 84); and also an explanation that, in fact, they can become true witnesses to everyone that marriage is indissoluble. Also, there is a recent brief but valuable study on the necessity of reassessing "spiritual communion" as a practice that can help those who cannot receive the Eucharist (Paul Josef Cardinal Cordes, *Spiritual Communion: The Eucharist for All*).

Finally, the Synod on the Family also insisted that pastoral care of these Christians in an irregular situation cannot be reduced to the question of receiving the Eucharist; rather, the pastors must try to welcome them with sensitivity and cordiality, to accompany them and integrate them in the regular life of the Church. That said, that pastoral accompaniment will always be rendered according to conscience and the teaching of the Church. On one hand, Saint John Paul II warned that being pastoral does not mean a compromise between the doctrine of the Church and the complex reality of daily life but, rather, leading individuals to Christ (*Veritatis splendor*, no. 56). On the other hand, the possible separation between individual conscience and the Magisterium of the Church would be analogous to separating pastoral practice from doctrine, along the lines of what was censured in a letter of the Congregation for the Doctrine of the Faith in 1994 regarding the consequences of an erroneous concept of conscience.

Some people say that the Church's position is not realistic and that it is better to adjust it to the present times. In that way the prophetic voice of the Church is silenced by "facts"; the gospel is presented as an "ideal" that, in the long run, cannot truly transform people's lives. What can we say about these opinions? What consequences would they have for our concept of the family?

The Church lives by God's truth and therefore is responsible to man for it. She bears witness to it with humility and with the strength that the Lord gives her, without allowing herself to be cowed by the world's accusations. On marriage and the sexual morality that she has received from God, she must remember the substantial unity of man in spirit, soul, and body, his relationship with the community, the truth about the totality of the gift required for sexuality to be human, the intergenerational responsibility, the identity as man and woman in their essential mutual reference.

These principles are not just an ideal, because love is never just an ideal, or even just a beautiful concept; it is instead a concrete dedication of life and the deep-rooted availability that opens the horizon of hope in individuals' daily lives.

All of us know that we are sinners and that it is in the sphere of sexuality that human weakness obviously manifests itself. But this does not mean that the sexual morality taught by the Church is an unattainable ideal. The biggest scandal of which the Church is capable is not that there should be sinners in her, but that she should stop explicitly calling the difference between good and evil by name and that she should relativize that difference, stop explaining what sin is, or try to justify it by a supposedly greater closeness to and mercy toward the sinner.

What hope can young people who are preparing themselves for marriage place in the Church? And what can young couples hope for from the Church? These questions will help us better understand another important question: What kind of pastoral transformation can they hope for from the Church? Or, better still, what kind of pastoral transformation does the Lord expect of the Church with respect to families?

Pope Francis has strongly emphasized this need for an authentic pastoral transformation of the Church. We must pay more attention to families and their problems. They need to be accompanied properly, to be able to rediscover and live their role as "domestic Church". Fathers and mothers need to receive a better education if we want them to be the "first evangelizers" of their children and their first school of life and faith, provided always that knowledge of the contents of the faith must be accompanied by the experience of a personal encounter with the Lord.

Catechesis in the parishes and the teaching of religion and morality in the schools, as well as the living testimony of those who have had that encounter with the Lord and transmit it in order to awaken the desire to follow him and serve him with all their heart and all their soul, are aimed at making it possible for the child and the adolescent to live the encounter with Christ. This requires a true pastoral conversion from everyone. It would be a big step forward if we were to learn that the family itself is not just a receiver of evangelization but is also a *subject* of the new evangelization. I dare say "the" subject of it.

What have we learned about all this in the two latest Synods on the Family? What general evaluation can we make? If we listen to what the media have said, we see that there is great internal tension in the Church.

The two latest synods have sent a decisive message: The family is the path of the Church, which must emerge from her self-referentiality and take that path resolutely. It is true, on the other hand, that there has been a certain tension, magnified by the media, which have failed to understand that this is normal and even necessary in such meetings.

It is essential that priests, catechists, and families themselves accept this path and this stimulus, in a dynamic of greater awareness of and regard for the doctrine of the

Church on the goodness and greatness of the family. But families, too, must bear witness to the fact that the Lord accompanies them and that, even in their frailties, God is faithful to his promises and works wonders in their lives. I therefore consider that these two latest synods have been, deep down, a call to all of us to accompany families, proposing to them the practices required to make family life possible in a new and difficult context.

Man's destiny hangs on whether he lives his capacity for love well. Everyone recognizes this. The Church adds that only a "true" love, manifested in the promise of "forever", fulfills man and allows him to attain his destiny, introducing him here and now into an experience of eternity. This truth allows spouses to build something bigger than themselves and understand that beyond their fragility there is an original love that sustains and regenerates and that, for that reason, forgiveness of each by the other is possible. This truth about love, genuine hope, is what the Church transmits today with humility and courage.

IV

WHAT CAN WE HOPE FOR FROM SOCIETY?

*Many questions arise under this heading, beginning with edu-
cation. What can we hope for from education? The university
is where the search for truth is conducted. The Scots philosopher
Alasdair MacIntyre said once that the university should not be a
"multiversity", alluding to the university's mission to watch over
the unity of knowledge, the unity of truth—that is, a truth that
gives unity to life and to society. Where has the university gone
astray? What are the paths to renewal? What does the university
have to do to offer a new vision of "everything"?*

The truth is one because God is one. But we men are
finite beings, and the truth appears to us in various
dimensions. Experience does not give us easily accessible
proof of what is true: we have to discern truth little by
little. The path of learning it is slow, penetrating step
by step and with great tenacity into the various dimensions in which truth appears in reality, such as empirical
truths, historical truths, philosophical truths, transcendental truths, and so on. Aristotle in his *Metaphysics* said that
every man naturally seeks the truth: in this sense, all of
us are philosophers—lovers of the truth—in one way or
another. The love of truth protects us from being reduced
to our political, economic, or ideological interests.

Why do we speak of the "university" instead of the "multiversity"? This institution has its origin in the Christian Middle Ages. In an extremely precarious environment but also with a great *catholic* or universal daring and spirit, medieval man, convinced of the *ratio divinae sapientiae*, organized and structured his search for truth in different faculties. Right from the beginning, then, the university united the different forms of knowledge and the sciences (*universitas scientiarum*) with the vision that, beyond its practical, technical, or economic ends, there existed a unique truth that calls to men. Obviously, every science had its own purposes and methods and its own utility, which contributed decisively to the betterment of human living conditions, but in the end all these were conceived of in terms of their service to the one great truth about man.

Therefore, the different sciences, without limiting truth to what can be verified by experimentation, allow the ordering of all knowledge to the truth and unicity of man, ultimately making possible the meeting of man and his Creator. In this sense, the method of scientific reasoning consists in analyzing the rational structure of matter. The question of the intersection of our spirit and that rational structure belongs, however, to two other sciences, philosophy and theology, both of them supremely necessary if we want to answer our fundamental questions, such as how to govern rationally, how to recognize what is just. The Church proposes that nature and reason, if they are grounded in the creative reason of God, can illuminate the *ethos* and, therefore, the law.

With scientific rigor, today as it did in its beginnings, the university finds the ultimate principle of unity in man, which makes possible the encounter with God. "Not to act 'with *logos*' is contrary to God's nature", Benedict XVI said in his lecture at Regensburg on September 12, 2006.

These centers of learning continue to be equally necessary today for society, and not only because of their utility in the preparation of students for the professions.

Let us offer an example: one can study the history of the Roman people, its culture, its organization, and its law purely as a pastime, which can seem to be more or less interesting. But in the university, we also seek to understand what are the laws of that history and what we can learn from them in order better to understand our world of today. One can also study a biography of Mozart for the simple pleasure of knowledge, but in the university one also seeks to deepen his understanding of this musical genius and of what lies behind his compositions, to discover the breadth and range of his music. Out of necessity or of love for the subject, we can learn on our own to organize a business or to understand the dynamics that generate wealth, but in the university we learn to do it in relation to other knowledge and for the overall good of man.

The great challenge of the university, therefore, is akin to the great challenge of education in general. We should see every child, adolescent, or youth as a person with a vocation for fulfillment, which he will only attain for himself but not by himself. He is someone who constantly needs help and company in order to develop the maturity he needs so that his education will serve his entire development and play its full part in his freedom and opening to the truth, when he is capable of embracing his origin and his destiny.

In that connection, we should consider that the ancients understood education as "leading out" or "bringing to light" what is hidden in every man. Perhaps it was possible in earlier times to take for granted that hidden fulfillment of man and how to attain it. Today, however, that approach to education is branded as paternalistic. But this modern prejudice can be a call not to consider education as a manipulation of mind or spirit or as training of the body and behavior or as a taming of emotions, as if they were simple instincts.

Educators are parents, siblings, school, teachers, and also the media, authors of books or articles, artists, athletes ... in this sense, a whole people or a community that takes pride in its traditions is an educator.

Our Western society is witnessing, however, the introduction of new stories with contradictory messages about what makes life great and beautiful. From elementary school to the university, instead of emphasizing as we used to what one should contribute to the common good, we value almost exclusively what one feels and what one can demand from others. And we exaggerate the value of scientific and technical information and tend to undervalue those disciplines which explore the great question about the meaning of things and of life.

Perhaps also because we have given up truly teaching, teaching the truth?

No doubt it is true that many of our educational centers have given up truly teaching. They look at their task from a "procedural" point of view—that is, teaching only the procedures that lead to discovering things by oneself. This has a certain value, because to educate is not to indoctrinate or manipulate or train. But the student asks for something more: he asks for evidence of the grandeur of life and the reasons for that grandeur; he asks to be shown where the truth lies and how to find it. Not to take on these questions in education is to abandon the student in a ship on the high seas, leaving him to navigate a totally uncertain course on his own, with no particular destination and without the real ability to deal with it, even if he is very well versed in the techniques of rowing.

Let us not forget that the media also educate, with their subliminal slogans in which a good end justifies clumsy means, and they raise false doubts that then give way to moral relativism. It is precisely the school and the university that should be ideal places in which to unmask the manipulation that comes with some of the models of life that are offered by the media. What is more, they should partner with parents in giving children and young people the means with which to assimilate their present and future tragedies, such as the drama of the broken marriage of their parents, the death of their grandparents, and the big moral decisions of the workplace.

All education should be aimed at interpreting life and embracing it in all its complexity and fragility. The educational fabric you mention should be based on this understanding, so we do not leave our children and young people to face their future alone.

Can a Catholic educator, who knows that there is an "inner Teacher", reduce education to a simple matter of method? What new horizon opens up to him with the possibility of channeling the inner Teacher?

A teacher knows from experience that he is dealing with a mystery: the mystery of a fulfillment to be attained, of a flowering of the individual that carries with it the discovery of the truth about his own destiny and of his orientation with maturity at each stage of his life. The teacher cannot force that, nor can he produce it himself: he can only accompany the individual and motivate him. This is the drama: it is not a given that the student will attain his fulfillment or flower in time.

That is how, in addressing the greatness of the vocation of each student, the true teacher understands his role of mediating the inner Teacher: the Holy Spirit. The whole effort of the educator, the whole task that he carries out with so much generosity and creativity for the good of the child, is the mediation of the greater task that the Spirit himself carries out in the heart of the student so that he will grow in every way. The mystery of how each person attains his fulfillment is the mystery of how the inner Teacher is allowed to act in him and how the outer teacher is used by the inner Teacher so that each individual will discover the truth and choose the good.

I therefore think that educating is much more than instructing, training, or developing skills. Nor can it consist of mere control or repression, with the risk of destabilization that that carries with it. To educate is to open the way to beauty and greatness in the child, in the adolescent, and in the youth. It is to show him the meaning of the moral law that he has inscribed in his heart, not as a requirement of society, but as a precondition of fulfillment. Of course, he does not understand that at the outset, because he believes that fulfillment is the satisfaction of his whims or opinions. The trust that a good teacher provides, however, allows him to develop his own vision little by little and understand the call to a greater love for the good, the beautiful, and the true.

Something similar happens with the commandments of the Church, such as going to Mass on Sunday: a youth can see them as an imposition by the Church or as a way to please his parents, even as a social requirement. The true teacher is one who shows him the demands he faces in pursuing his own fulfillment as an encounter with Jesus who has given his life for him and who awaits him in Mass to continue giving him life. If we help him overcome his laziness, organize his time, especially on Saturday night, he will see that time which he gives to Jesus as something that lends vitality to his whole week.

But the Church has been accused of "paternalism" when she attempts to educate the affectivity of children and young people. Is that justified? Is the education of affectivity the product of a true paternity, or is it a derivative of that hyper-protection characteristic of "paternalism"? How should affectivity be educated? Is it not precisely in hope and the vocation to love, in the capacity to receive and embrace another person as a person?

A person cannot be just an "object" of education, because every child and adolescent is a person, a "subject" endowed with a profound mystery, a creature of God who, in his dignity, can never be made into a tool. This is the first principle that every educator must respect: certainty about the magnitude of what is at stake. If he does, the child will be able to understand that, looking beyond the work that is required of him and the things he does not yet understand, the education he receives is not aimed at mistreating or controlling him but, rather, at opening him little by little to a new and constantly widening horizon. That way, education turns into an interesting adventure!

Given the deficit in parenthood, which is in turn a reflection of the serious educational problem that affects man today, we must remember and insist that to be a parent is to have a passion for initiation into what we call life in capital letters. It is to point his child to his life's horizon, accompanying him with wisdom from his first steps and respecting him in his uniqueness. It is therefore to avoid the paternalism of giving him everything ready-made, as a substitute for the arduous work of making his own way.

To be a parent and teacher involves assuming unambiguous authority, which opens paths and broadens horizons, which also knows how to be serious and does not operate according to the taste and whim of the student. This work is the most complicated that an adult can ever do: it requires integrity, strength, courage, tenderness, closeness, loyalty, trust, and above all a great deal of patience. The parent who takes seriously his task as an educator does not try first and at all cost to "be likable" to his child. Surprisingly, couples need to be reminded of this often because there is always a temptation that one or the other will present himself as the sympathetic and lenient one, allowing the other to be the rigid and repressive one. Any parent must in his own way insist on the basics and the good. Tenaciously, because no one learns to speak another language or play an instrument with pleasure, especially at the beginning. Good parents are always there, in good times and bad.

Your question also touches on what is today an essential point: the education of affectivity and sexuality. In many countries, the laws of education treat sex education as mere information, left in the hands of "experts"—that is, teachers of natural science, who explain how sexuality functions from the point of view of biology and health, with the practical objective of avoiding the problems of hygiene, disease, or unwanted pregnancy. This avoids the question of meaning and causes the educational failure that we observe with such perplexity.

Throughout my years of priestly ministry, however, I have been able to see that what young people want is precisely to discover the meaning of sex, its relationship to love, its opening to the future. For that reason, emotional-sexual education is a duty that begins at the first moment of the child's life and that, unavoidably and definitively, falls on the parents. They can be supported, but they cannot be supplanted, by school and other educational institutions like the parish.

What would sex education consist of, specifically, today? Without attempting an exhaustive answer, I believe that it is in any case a matter of helping an adolescent interpret his emotional experiences: he should develop the ability to interpret his affections and feelings with a view to where they are taking him, revealing to him the truth that lies hidden in them. But it is not enough simply to interpret, either: adolescents and young people need our help in integrating this great variety of feelings, some of them passionate, that they experience, revealing to them the underlying desires and helping lead them back to the truth that is recognizable in them. That is the way to generate the virtue that is appropriate to lovers: chastity.

Our youth have a hard time with their sexuality because our society does not live in the truth: they are not taught to respect their body and their person as instruments that God has given us to live true love; they are not introduced to modesty; they are not protected from being reduced, as many will try to reduce them, to mere objects and tools. Our adolescents, facing the challenges of the times in which we live, need someone, starting with their parents, to reveal to them the perennial newness of the gospel, so that they will be educated in current language and by relevant and effective means that do not adulterate the Christian message. This work will surely be easier if these same young people discover other young people who are disposed to take this same road: for that, the world meetings of youth and all the pastoral work with youth in the diocese and parish that revolves around them are important. In this environment they do not feel like strangers or a marginal minority; instead, they are motivated to continue maturing in the company of Christ. We urgently have to answer to these educational needs that are characteristic of very complicated stages of attaining our personal maturity.

I am touching here on the question, so close to Benedict XVI's heart, of the educational emergency in our society: in his lecture to the Italian bishops on the occasion of the 65th Plenary Assembly on May 27, 2010, the now pope emeritus explored the consequences for education of a false idea of man's autonomy and of the current skeptical and relativist culture, which silences nature, revelation, and history, considering this last an agglomeration of arbitrary cultural decisions that are not valid for either the present or the future. Regarding what anti-authoritarian education aspires to do, he declared that it is a true renunciation of education, because the "I", the incomplete being created by the dialogue, must seek fulfillment, not in itself, but rather only in the encounter with the "thou" and the "you". The pope emeritus also said it would be fundamental to recover the concept of nature as the "Creation of God that speaks to us" and of revelation as "deciphering" the book of creation, "in which God gives us our fundamental orientation" to reveal a history that is substantially valid.

Pope Francis, for his part, has also said repeatedly that the matter of education is a priority of our society, demanding that parents return to being protagonists of education. On November 21, 2015, he said to the participants in a world congress on education: "To educate is to introduce into the totality of truth."

Let us turn to another subject regarding social life. Let us talk about poverty. It is not an easy problem to solve. Pope Francis has repeatedly made it evident that this is one of the great plagues of our modern societies and that it must be addressed with solidarity, as a whole, not with sector-by-sector solutions. He says in Evangelii gaudium *(no. 67) that the great poverty that limits the development of societies is individualism—the poverty in relationships. If we do not create a true network of relationships among individuals, we will repeat the experience of the consumerist West. What can we hope for from our society in this regard? Shouldn't we take the route of generating and strengthening social relationships so as to bring into being a true social fabric that will facilitate the search for solutions?*

Here, too, we find ourselves facing another form of dualism: the distinction between material poverty and spiritual poverty. Something like "first we have to do away with material poverty, and then we can take up other questions." That way, fundamental subjects like culture, education, and even the worship of God are relegated to being secondary matters to be considered last.

This form of dualism is erroneous because it breaks up and disintegrates human reality. Man is a material entity and, at the same time, a person who lives in society as embodied spirit. Essential dimensions of the human being like the religious element or the cultural aspect cannot be curtailed or relegated to our spare time. We cannot fall into false puritanism or pauperism—thinking, for example, that every expenditure on culture or art is a superfluous luxury. For us to reach our personal destiny, everyone with whom we come into contact, including the poor, must share, not just the basic things required for survival, but share what will enable them to meet all their legitimate needs as individuals, thereby having access to cultural and spiritual goods that will enhance their humanity.

The misery that originates in the lack of the staples of life, such as food, drink, clothing, housing, education, participation in politics and public life in general, should be fought and conquered, because it is an expression of a social sin, which is sometimes structural, a consequence in turn of original sin. That situation arises when a group or an elite serves its own interests, so that they can selfishly enjoy the pleasures that come with luxury and wealth, from the goods that should belong to all and be devoted to the common good. These sinful phenomena demand a solution grounded not in ideology but in justice.

The Church must always be very alert against allowing herself to be seduced by a secularized conception of social action that, in its ambiguity, is always mistaken, because authentic evangelization of the person is always integral. In that regard, Pope Francis has said in his apostolic exhortation *Evangelii gaudium* (no. 200) that it is not a matter of lending aid to the poor as a "philanthropic" exercise or introducing them into a materialist and consumerist logic: "The worst discrimination which the poor suffer is the lack of spiritual care." And I remember that, in his very first homily as pope, he issued the warning that if we do not confess to Jesus Christ, the Church stops being what she is and becomes a charitable NGO.

What can we hope for from the economy? The subject of the common good, of course, which is so frequently forgotten, gives us a central point of reference. In the management of a nation's resources, the test of the common good is decisive, as Pope Francis constantly reminds us. Beyond the ingenuous vision of economic resources as a gift that must be put to use, it is necessary to understand not only how they are generated but also that the use to which they are devoted is determined by the mode of their generation. In this sense, might it not be helpful in understanding the generation and use of resources to take into account that the family is the greatest social capital? That would be to conceive of the family as the basic social capital of a nation, the source of wealth and development. Could we then consider the economy in the context of the social value to which other structures and social fabrics contribute?

We have to have a good understanding of the term "social capital" to avoid falling into the use of some categories that are not applicable to people. It seems to me that you are talking here about the family as social capital insofar as the family generates those social virtues that only it can produce. In the family, made up of persons but not of individuals, one learns that personal happiness depends on the happiness of others. By providing an education in relationships and, therefore, in the generous inclusion of others, the family becomes the privileged environment in which to discover the visceral, deep empathy that God experiences for every one of us: that God who never tires of bridging the infinite gap between himself and our sinful ego. In our own family we are loved unconditionally, learning therefrom God's way of loving. Our families provide us with the necessary antibodies against all selfishness and expediency.

Personal virtues become social virtues in the family. There its members learn to cultivate and express their humanity in other social settings. Because of the stability and cohesion that the family gives its members, it is the fundamental fabric of society in the economy as well and, in fact, is the true source of the wealth of any nation. In that connection, Gary Stanley Becker (*Human Capital: A Theoretical and Empirical Analysis, with Special Reference to Education*), winner of the Nobel Prize in Economics in 1992 and an expert in relating microeconomic analysis to behavior and human interaction, insisted for years that the family is the foundation for increasing the efficiency of the process by which a nation generates wealth. He wondered: Why do we seek to produce and exchange goods? The answer is simple: We have needs and seek to satisfy them by making a profit, so whatever satisfies a need acquires value and generates wealth. Since resources are limited, man seeks efficiency, maximizing his well-being, while society, for its part, seeks to maximize its utility. Becker therefore emphasized that, along with land, work, and capital, the fourth and most relevant factor in production is human capital—that is, all the human skills and qualities that a person has when he is born and that he accumulates all his life to work more efficiently and productively. The family is therefore the basic and fundamental human organization, because it is where the greatest investment of human capital is made in areas such as health, education, and the well-being of children, and at a very low cost, given the perfect altruism of its members. If a society grows or is developed without making an adequate investment in human capital, without reciprocal trust, without the capacity for teamwork, without a readiness to forgive, without a generous helpfulness, all of which are learned in the family, how will that society be able to subsist?

Pope Francis has himself often criticized the interpretation of capitalism that maintains that the center and basic hermeneutic of human existence is not the person, but capital. He has not criticized the free market system or capital as such, because he understands that they are key elements of the modern globalized economy, unlike other economic models of antiquity based on the exchange of products. In reality, the objects of the pope's criticism are certain principles that go beyond the simple economic regulation of the market and that, according to him, are a great challenge for our democracies. He is talking, on the one hand, about the selfish, radically individualist, and profoundly irresponsible attitude of a small financial and business elite that causes social destabilization. This elite tends to concentrate more and more wealth, going from incomes in the 1950s, for example, that were twenty times more than a middle-level employee's to incomes that now are two hundred times more. On the other hand, and in this his analysis is very incisive, the pope is also talking about the factors that make that possible: in the absence of adequate political and ethical counterweights, this elite ends up concentrating political power as well, so that it can influence and manipulate in its favor the rules that govern the national economy, thereby avoiding self-regulation of the market with the aim of broadly diffusing prosperity, thus denying citizens an equitable distribution of the wealth that has been generated by all.

This analysis, which should in principle be solely economic, ultimately raises the profound crisis that affects our democratic institutions, the growing lack of trust in them and the resultant weakening of the social fabric, which has been pointed out by the philosopher John Rawls, among others. It is only from these premises that one can understand Francis' call to live authentic social virtues that break radically with this logic and enable us to think in terms of an economy that works in solidarity with the most disfavored and is responsible in its use of the resources of our planet. Thus in *Laudato si* (no. 211), he affirms that "only by cultivating sound virtues will people be able to make a selfless ecological commitment. A person who could afford to spend and consume more but regularly uses less heating and wears warmer clothes, shows the kind of convictions and attitudes which help to protect the environment."

Besides these premises regarding the capitalist system, the Church insists that the conduct of business affairs and the management of companies must be ethically correct, not because that will itself be profitable, though it is that, too, but above all because the economy regulates personal relationships. Our businesses should again be centered on man, who is created by God as his son and destined for a life that is consistent with his worth. For that, we would have to return to ethical practices among all the productive members of society that would compensate them fairly for their work, respect established norms, and value quality, honesty, and effort, among other things.

All of this, I repeat, comes together in the family, which is our first lesson in the common good and the first social unit that generates social capital: because this social reality is a good that is itself indivisible and has its own transcendent meaning beyond the sum of the individual goods of its components, when it is properly valued by all of a nation's social actors, it permits a correct configuration of the global economic and political reality (*Catechism of the Catholic Church*, no. 1910).

What can we hope for from society? It seems as though the Christian outreach to all has run up against a society in which the "Christian fact" has come to occupy a more and more marginal space. In response to this question, Pope Emeritus Benedict XVI, in his visit to the Czech Republic, referred to the Church as a "creative minority". With that reference he took up again the solution that the historian Arnold Toynbee gave for the problem of a culture's decline. He said that, to overcome decline, creative minorities must emerge in society and confront the crisis with a new intelligence. But do such minorities exist today?

With the concept of a "creative minority", Arnold J. Toynbee (*A Study of History*) was referring to historical situations in which great changes originated in the passing of one civilization and the rise of another. In circumstances like those, while some were clinging to a past that was disappearing and others were fleeing into the future, losing the heritage of the past they had known, creative minorities were emerging that were capable of making the transition between the old and the new.

The reality of the "creative minority" that is capable of serving as the yeast of a society is therefore not simply a reality of today. It has been present in the Church throughout her history. We have many examples of it: in the days of Saint Teresa of Ávila, there were certainly many monks and nuns in Spain, but Christianity frequently lacked vigor. One could say that it was a self-satisfied Christianity, too secularized and worldly. A small minority of saints, however, seeded the Church in Spain with new vitality and made it possible for her to transfigure the whole society of her time, welcoming the new of the period without breaking with the great ecclesial tradition of the past. Without the prophetic voice of that creative minority, the Church of Spain's Golden Age would not have been able to recognize, as she did at the time, the role that Jesus played in her history.

A conformist minority can never be a creative minority. Saint Pius X chose as his motto "Restore all things in Christ" (see Eph 1:10). This pope, like his predecessors Pius IX and Leo XIII, had as one of the great obstacles to his ministry the "Roman question"—that is, the lack of material sustenance for the Holy See after the loss of the Papal States. Despite that, he saw his pontificate as a universal mission, the absolute opposite of closing himself up in a comfortable ivory tower. He understood that, as a minority, Christianity should not settle for just the external or ritual, but instead should take on the great challenge of being creative in society from a new personal relationship with Christ.

The creative minority, which is the opposite of the "masses", is a profoundly evangelical concept. Let us recall the images of the minuscule in the Gospels: the seed, the grain of mustard, yeast ... The Kingdom of Heaven is presented in Jesus' preaching as this tiny reality that nevertheless is capable of generating something great. Salt and the lamp that was small but, even so, lit up the whole room are other examples of the same thing. It is always a matter of the power of the small and fragile, the capacity of the seed to bear fruit.

We see examples of this in some European nations, especially in those with Slavic culture whose Catholicism permeates broad layers of the population thanks to their tenacious and martyr-like resistance to the seductions of materialism. In places like Poland or Croatia, border countries and veterans of the European tragedy of the twentieth century, being a Catholic today is a mark of national identity, but it has also recently been a reason for their exclusion, marginalization, and even persecution. In that connection, the Blessed Cardinal Alojzije Stepinać, Archbishop of Zagreb, who took as his episcopal motto *In te Domine speravi*, prophetically declared—shortly before he died after the martyrdom to which he was subjected by the new Communist regime in his country between 1946 and 1960—that a state based exclusively on materialist principles could not endure. On another occasion, when he was being interrogated during his confinement in Krašić regarding his activity as a pastor under surveillance, he said he simply did his duty: "To suffer and work for the Church".

This glory of the noble Croatian people, a man of deep faith and a saint who acted out his faith in an exceptional way in his life and work (cf. Benedict XVI, *Verbum Domini* 48), revealed to us that even in the most problematic political situation, if we belong to the creative Christian minority, we can find in God the grace and consolation we need in order to make the most correct decision, to endure adversities, to forgive our enemies, and even to illuminate the rest of society with manifestations of real hope. Today, there may be unavailing attempts to vilify and calumniate this giant figure, reopening the wounds of his martyrdom, but I think this may be the path that Providence has traced for us to keep his memory alive and accelerate the full recognition of the sanctity of this exemplary pastor. Any good man will be impressed by his commitment to the truth, the honesty with which he lived, and his service to reconciliation, also in the field of ecumenism. We Catholics, however, beyond admiring him, are called as well to communion of life, of prayer, and of worship with him. In this regard, I hope that his sepulchral urn in the presbytery of Zagreb Cathedral will become an important destination of international pilgrimage that will attract many faithful, especially pastors, who pray and honor this martyr to freedom of conscience and the exercise of pastoral charity.

We Christians are permanently on the path and always in the minority, not in the sociological sense, but rather in the ecclesiological sense—that is, as salt of the earth and light to the world, like anyone who is called to give flavor to life and shine on all men.

The Christian method has never been directly a method of the "masses", has always been to act as yeast, as a grain of mustard. What is it that makes a parish, a group, a movement, an ecclesial reality multiply? By what marks can we recognize the minority?

It is important, first of all, to remember that Christianity has never admitted classes of Christians, in the sense that *gnosis* understands it—that is, as if there were a chosen few, a minority of the perfect graced with special and exclusive gifts, which constitutes the spiritual elite. Christianity has always admitted that there are different speeds and intensities in the Christian life, because it is a development that progresses in stages, on a path that includes falls. By that I mean that groups that live a very intense life in the parish or the movement should never succumb to the temptation to separate themselves from the rest, as though they were the ecclesial aristocracy compared to those who live more at a distance. They should always understand their involvement as grace for others, a means, not for glorifying themselves, but for placing themselves at the service of the rest.

You ask me now for the marks by which we may recognize the fertility of a "creative minority". I would say, first and foremost, that those marks are not a simple commodity and that they are recognized only by those eyes which know how to look beyond the pure appearance of a result or a series of numbers.

Love is the unmistakable sign of that fertility: not a passing feeling, but a love that has matured and therefore has become a virtue—that is, a habit acquired through an apprenticeship, having repeated certain acts that develop those operative potentialities in man that enable him to do good and to do well what has to be done.

The other virtues characteristic of a creative minority will be, in any case, the virtues that keep it united: trust, the sense of belonging, joy, generosity, the recognition of the superabundance of what has been received, gratitude, the responsibility required to work and build together. A creative minority can be recognized wherever hospitality and the embrace of diversity are alive, avoiding both the ghetto and the bunker as well as the trench.

Other virtues of that minority are those which are characteristic of all that is creative, such as audacity, magnanimity, and the humility that recognizes the greatness of God.

Together with this "minority" that, as you have just said, is creative in love and service, there is also a sad reality that appears in our Church. It is found in places or institutions where the most that can be done is to "manage decline": supervise the closure of parishes, minimize the damage done by the lack of priests, sell off seminaries and church buildings, administer the transfer of religious schools that their own congregations can no longer keep going ... That is, doing what is necessary to soften the fall, to maintain the appearance of a presence in society. What are the marks by which we recognize decline?

First of all, true decline does not consist in the fact that parishes and seminaries are emptier now. This is a situation that causes a great deal of sadness and is, in itself, a bad symptom. The true illness, the decline that I fear more, relates to those inner attitudes that contaminate our hearts. I mean seeing Christianity as an archeological site, choosing to live an enclosed life, rambling among the ruins of a distant past, no matter how glorious, like the cats in the Roman forum. At other times, it will consist in resigning oneself to enduring the present moment with that sadness which can never come from Christ. In other cases, some people mistakenly think that keeping faith with their own principles implies an aggressive attitude against all attempts to renew faith, hope, and love. These are forms of Christianity that are, certainly, in decline.

This decline always has its origin in a lack of trust in God's plan for his Church. For anyone who loves the Church and has given her his entire life, it is very sad to see so many couples who, when they are faced with the first difficulties of their conjugal life, decide not to keep struggling and therefore start a new relationship from zero and break off the preceding one. It is saddening, too, to see so many "burned-out" priests, who after a prolonged period of great difficulty in the living of their ministry appear to be always stressed out and tired of everything and everyone, apathetic, bewildered, and sometimes overcome by the lack of understanding on the part of someone who should be like a father to them, their bishop. All of these are clear signs of decline that are much more telling than falling numbers.

There is only one way to overcome it: by clearly affirming that our only hope is in Jesus Christ. Human sociology, with its data and statistics, need not frighten us or make us lose faith. How often, in other times, has the Church been in situations like ours! And the Church has always felt the consoling presence of the Spirit. In the time of the Roman Empire, the emperors, the philosophers, and the important members of that society were convinced that Christianity was the religion for fools, slaves, and lower-class people, an encumbrance to progress and an embarrassment to humanity. Remember the period of the Lutheran reform, when priests heard it said that the Mass was idolatry, that the priesthood did not exist, that the whole hierarchy was an abuse, that the sacrament of ordination was a demoniac rite. Think of their despair when they saw many of their faithful adopting these ideas. Or think of the French Revolution, too, when the people rushed to persecute priests and religious, considered by many to be parasites and enemies of society on account of their supposedly antiquated and harmful ideas.

In short, there have been attacks against the Church throughout history. And so there are today, too. We will decline only if these situations make us lose hope and lead us to resign ourselves and merely manage the present.

Chesterton said that one of the factors of decline was blind trust in technology. I suggest other factors for your consideration: the lack of creativity, the interest in doing nothing more than "apply Band-Aids", plug holes, settle cases . . . So the direction in which we are going does not matter as long as the ship stays afloat.

Yes, we could describe these and may other signs of decline. Of course, one of the clearest signs of it lies in the difficulty of integrating and assimilating what is different. Life, even in its most basic biological aspects, consists in our capacity to metabolize diversity and make it our own. That is what the Blessed J. H. Cardinal Newman says, the exceptional Englishman who was always ready to be transformed by the truth. In his *Essay on the Development of Christian Doctrine*, he writes that decline sets in when we are metabolized by the external, when it is we who are assimilated because we lack the resources necessary to be the assimilator. The fundamental problem that all these cases reflect is parsimony, mediocrity, short-sightedness, and the loss of the virtue that is characteristic of every creative minority: magnanimity.

Let me suggest that we turn now to considering another point of view, perhaps a more positive one. Guareschi describes how on the banks of the Po, when the river crested in a flood, the peasants could save very few things from their houses, moving them to the upper floors so that the rising waters would not destroy them. Those peasants did not hesitate: what they saved was the seed of the next crop. It was the seed of faith. They knew that, with

*that seed, they had a future, they would be able to sow a crop the
following year. What is the seed we need to save today? What
dangers do substitutes for that seed pose for us, as if we could
guarantee our future with them?*

The seed we must move to the upper floors in this time
of aggressive laicism is faith in Christ as the living Son of
God. This is the only seed that matters, if we truly are
interested in assuring the future of the generations that
follow us: faith in Christ, together with the sacraments.
What did the English Catholics do during the three hundred years of legislation that prohibited Catholicism as a
crime? What did Christians do during the terrible persecutions in China and Japan? What did they save? Their faith
in Jesus Christ, manifested in the personal witness they
bore by their life in communion with the whole Church
and by their love for the Bible and the books on the lives
of the saints, for they were role models they could imitate,
who would sustain them in their tribulations. What saved
the Christians in the Nazi concentration camps or forced-
labor camps or in the Soviet Gulag? In large part, it was
their faith, for without that they lost all hope: the priests
tried to celebrate the Eucharist whenever they could, even
under very extraordinary conditions. It was the center
of their encounter with Christ. Yes: what saved them was
the intimacy of their sacramental encounter with Christ.
On other occasions, when it was not physically possible to
receive the sacrament bodily, they nourished their personal
piety and received the consolation they needed by uniting
themselves with him in spirit, offering yet another historic
example of "spiritual communion" as an excellent remedy
that makes it possible to receive the Lord fruitfully.

   "The seed is the word of God" (Lk 8:11). There are other
words in our lives; in fact, we are seeing an inflation of

empty words. There are other promises that are nothing but substitutes. The parable of the wheat and the weeds (see Mt 13:24–52) explains to us that the good seed is sown with the weeds. The latter grow together with the true Word, but they bear no fruit because they are barren. The weeds can be clearly recognized only at harvest time, but while the crop is ripening they grow together. But the weeds do not guarantee the future: in the end, they are the straw of worries, of appetites, activism, which are borne away by the wind. The weeds are this collection of empty words, which bear no relation to the fruit that is generated by the Word in people's hearts. The key is to be aware of it and to struggle to grow the wheat until it is time for it to be harvested.

Is multiculturalism an option? In one very accurate statement, Joseph Ratzinger reminded us that Christianity has always been inculturated and that therefore no authentic process of inculturation of the gospel can take as its starting point a neutral, a-cultural gospel, which can later take distinct shape according to the culture. It is impossible, for example, to strip the gospel of Jewish culture, understand the sacrament of the Eucharist without reference to Passover, or present Christianity without reference to the dialogue with Greek culture. Joseph Ratzinger preferred to speak of interculturality. Many questions come up here: Can there be a Christianity that, stripped of its patristic era, returns to the pure gospel? Or, even more: Can there be a Christianity that is detached from all its medieval baggage, all of Scholasticism and also of the Council of Trent?

Actually, the word "inculturation" seems to me to be a bit off the mark, because it suggests that culture should be considered alongside the Incarnation, as though the latter were an incomplete act until it entered into each culture.

The Incarnation occurred once and only once in history: it consisted of the unique, hypostatic union of the divine and human nature in the *Logos*, the Second Person of the Holy Trinity, in a specific, known moment. The Incarnation of the Son of God, by virtue of its being integral and concrete, was a cultural fact in the history of the people of Israel.

The dialogue with other cultures therefore cannot be defined in any way as an "incarnation" parallel to the only Incarnation of the Word. Nor can it be a continuation of the Incarnation, for the purpose of completing it. That dialogue can only be conducted on the basis of the universalization of the event of Christ.

To answer your question specifically, I believe we should consider two aspects. First, the transcendence of revelation with respect to the cultures in which it is expressed: the Word of God is not identified exclusively with the culture in which it is transmitted. The gospel always assumes the conversion of the reader, and, in fact, it is strong enough to purify and amend the cultural elements. The gospel has also purified Jewish culture of its outdated and transient elements.

On the other hand, the gospel already exists in one culture, which it does not renounce although it does transcend it. Although it has to enter into cultures by establishing a continuing dialogue with all of them, it is always good news lived in the Church and linked to a specific cultural tradition, the Judeo-Christian one, from which it should be read and interpreted. For that reason, an avowed "evangelization of cultures" cannot consist of inserting the soul of the gospel into the body of a culture: as I said before, this theology of incarnation does not properly explain the process by which a culture is evangelized. Nor is it theologically acceptable for the dialogue with the various cultures to carry with it a renunciation of its historic baggage, of the body in which it has been transmitted, of its tradition.

I mentioned the people of Croatia and Poland before, but I believe Hungary is also an eminent example of a people that has a first-rate cultural tradition that has been shaped by the Christian event, in the wake of the conversion to Catholicism in the year 1000 of King Vajk, who adopted the name of the protomartyr Stephen. Thanks to the tireless work of great missionaries like Saint Adelbert of Prague, the conversion of Hungary not only transformed its pagan cultural tradition into the admirable Magyar culture that we know today and in fact made it possible for its royal dynasty to give the Church more saints than any other Catholic royal house, but also set in motion many forms of Eastern European Christian culture by making the most of the Danube, the main artery of communication between East and West. As an example, I would like to cite the sixth chapter of the *Instruction of Saint Stephen to His Son Emeric* (*Scriptores Regnum Hungaricarum II*), in which, as the exponent of the old barbarian Magyar tribal society, the king advises his son, once he has converted to Christianity, to welcome foreigners and strangers to his kingdom, "for a kingdom is weak and fragile if it has only one language and tradition."

Going back to the question, would it not be useful to start by asking what culture is?

It is not an easy concept to define, because it is not a simple sum of external characteristics. I would say that, first, it is language, because this not only is a tool for expressing ideas but embodies an entire way of thinking.

Second, culture is any means of expressing, realizing, and moving the human spirit. In that sense, culture includes other exterior forms like art and everything related to it: music, painting, architecture, bodily expression … So living in a solidly built house is different from being exposed to the elements in a flimsy shack. Architecture provides man with shelter, but it is also an expression of his dignity and esthetic sensibility. In all art forms, man expresses his experiences, his intentions, his dreams, his utopias, which are no less than the representation of his inner cosmos.

Culture is also the entire ambit of social relationships. All the ways of expressing the love of one's neighbor are culture, as when we struggle to help the poor and destitute improve their living conditions and, along with them, their dignity, rather than allowing them to be abandoned to their fate. That is how a legitimate social and political culture is generated. In that connection, in my many years of living in Peru, I have always been surprised by the enormous social culture that characterizes the peasant Quechua communities of the Andean *altiplano*, especially in relation to the elderly, to ancestors, and to living in harmony with creation.

Their political culture also allows for debate regarding the various options in a climate of mutual respect. It is legitimate for a politician to win elections, not for the purpose of suppressing opponents, but rather to work for the common good and thereby build a more just society. It is legitimate for the political opposition to show its disagreement, provided they use means that are legitimate under the rule of law and work with the government as a loyal opposition.

Culture, then, is a reality that is intrinsically open, which is derived from relationships among the people and, above all, with God. It is a preeminent characteristic of culture that we live in peace and are capable of mastering our immediate desires, trying thereby to make the world more livable, a veritable *domus*, or home, in which everyone feels at ease. Culture therefore goes beyond the knowledge that a person has been able to accumulate during his lifetime, because even that knowledge is subordinate to the possibility that that person, while recognizing that his dignity originated in his divine filiation, is the master of his own existence.

This may give us a better understanding of your reservation about the term "inculturation" and take us as well to the next question: Through what portal can the gospel and the Church of Christ enter the cultural dialogue?

Culture, as I just said, cannot be thought of as a static receptacle, as though Christianity were the contents of a bottle that could be poured from one vessel to another, from one culture to another. Christianity, however, has existed since its very inception in a specific human culture in which the Word was spoken.

When we insist on the "inculturation of the gospel", we could be giving an insufficient understanding of the fact that the gospel is already inculturated and is inseparable from the culture that gave birth to it. The gospel is therefore inseparable from the history of the Jewish people and from symbols as concrete as bread, wine, the laying on of hands, anointment with oil, and so on.

For the sake of argument, however, we need to reflect, even if only briefly, on the concept of revelation. This concept implies, first, that it is not possible to separate the *God who speaks* from the *man who hears the Word*. As a young theologian, Joseph Ratzinger wrote his post-doctoral habilitation thesis on just this subject, on the concept of revelation in Saint Bonaventure. The future pope demonstrated in that thesis that for Saint Bonaventure, the content of revelation was not static but dynamic, in the sense that it also implicated the hearer of the Word, to whom the Word is addressed. The thesis he defended could be summarized as follows: Without man as the recipient of the Word, an essential living subject, there cannot be any revelation of God. The German language itself echoes this conclusion, when we analyze the parallel between the term "word" (*Wort*) and the term "answer" (*Antwort*). Between the divine *Wort* and the human *Antwort*, we can see a reciprocity and a certain circularity.

It is the person of Christ that, in a unique and unsurpassable way, joins the Word of God to its expression in the human word. We can say that we are capable of hearing the Word of God precisely because we have the ears of Jesus Christ.

This short digression helps us address the answer to your question. Any truly cultural dialogue must begin with man as the "hearer of the Word", open to revelation. Christ is incarnated in the beginning, which made possible with his coming the fruitful dialogue between God and man. Therefore, when I understand what the Bible says, when I embrace the revelation of God, that is not a merely human act but, rather, one in which I hear with the ear of Christ and embrace the Word because I am lifted up by the Spirit of Christ.

Revelation takes place in a specific human culture and through a specific human response: specifically, the response of Judeo-Christian culture. But we may ask ourselves: What happens in the case of cultures that historically have nothing to do with the fact of Christianity? Through what portal can the gospel enter into them?

These other cultures always have seeds of the Word: it is always possible to single out in them a man who is searching for God, is disposed to venerate him, to dedicate his life to him, to understand that his life and destiny are in the hands of a higher power. All cultures have an opening to transcendence, made perceptible in rituals and even in codes of ethics. All these rites and religious expressions have defective elements, so they need to be purified, but they are genuine seeds of the unique truth of the gospel.

The mission of the Church is not at all to impose one culture on another. Although some are predisposed to present it that way, it is never a form of colonization founded on a feeling of superiority. The mission is where cultures meet in a way that calls for purification or fulfillment of what are no more than seeds of a reality that was not self-contained. In fact, an enclosed, self-contained culture would be an anti-culture. By its very nature, culture is open to others, wants to go beyond the small territory of its own family, its own hamlet, wants to escape from provincialism. This substratum of humanness, shared as a common heritage, is precisely what makes the mission possible.

It is therefore important to emphasize the need to avoid reducing Christianity to an ahistorical, incorporeal project. We cannot try to purify Christianity, to reduce it to an ahistorical, acultural, neutral essence, suitable for mass consumption. The model of the mission *ad gentes* cannot be that: in the dialogue that Christianity establishes with all cultures, the fulfillment of its universal vocation is at stake, when everyone, in a wondrous and astonishing phenomenon of communion, can understand each other through the workings of the Holy Spirit.

It follows that evangelization is a cultural phenomenon of the first order—I mean, one that implies the transformation of the culture.

But what elements of Christianity can somehow be "adapted" in this dialogue with other cultures?

We cannot take the view that, for the sake of a supposed "inculturation", Jesus should be presented on Palm Sunday riding an elephant instead of a donkey (to give a really striking example), that the Eucharist should appear in the form of typical local foods, instead of bread and wine. Evangelization involves entering into the culture of bread and wine, because Jesus established the Eucharist, not with abstract symbols, but with specific cultural symbols.

The Gospels should obviously be translated into the various languages, but always paying careful attention to the content of the translations. We cannot say, for example, that Jesus is God's nephew. He is the Son, and this concept expresses a very specific relationship. Nor can we hide his death on the Cross because we think it would have too harsh or scandalous an impact in a certain culture; and notice that this may already be happening in our politically correct Western world, this overly harsh or scandalous impact. Jesus died nailed to a Cross, subjected to the horrible tortures that we know about from the Gospels. This historical fact cannot be hidden or changed: it can be explained according to the pedagogy that is suitable for each milieu; rather, the message of the gospel must be given whole, initiating people into the new Christian culture.

Evangelization cannot be thought of in abstract form, based only on a few moral ideas and religious principles, because Christianity is based on a specific, historic, universal fact. To accept the gospel, it is necessary to enter and explore the culture of the Old Testament, understand the meaning of God's covenant with Abraham and the other patriarchs, the meaning of worship in Israel, the meaning of the Jewish *Pesach*, the jeremiads of the prophets and the kingdom of David. All of these and more are also cultural elements that exegetes must study in depth and make known to all, because they are part of the specific Christian universal.

V

CONCLUSION

THE KEY TO AN
UNDERSTANDING OF MERCY

With great vision, Pope Francis has declared a Year of Mercy. This presents us with a more authentically Christian view of the face of God. What does it mean to say that God is mercy?

I think, first, that sacramental confession is the most paradigmatic expression of God's mercy. This sign of grace enables us to understand how the Lord looks upon our sins. The way he looks at us in this sacrament, his just and at the same time good gaze, that gaze which does not abandon us in the quagmire of our miseries, that gaze which at the same time entails taking us seriously, becomes our gaze, for if God gives us a great deal, he also demands a great deal from us, knowing that we can give a great deal if we receive so much from him. Yes: God takes us seriously, but he does so like a good father who is able to be patient with his children, who never tires in accompanying them, and who, above all, never abandons them.

It is very important today to understand that both mercy and justice derive from divine goodness as their common source. There is a certain view of reality today that inflates the affective and the sentimental, in an attempt to convince us that mercy and justice are contradictory. But "Mercy and faithfulness will meet; righteousness and peace will kiss each other" (Ps 85:10), which is to say that, for God, to say justice is to say mercy, without contradiction.

In fact, it is impossible to understand God's mercy without taking justice into consideration. This is not some kind of scale on which I play at weighing my virtues and my faults against each other: it is not that because we know that God does not seek us out for our virtues or reject us for our faults. Nor does he measure us with a ruler or according to legal criteria external to him, by simply applying the Decalogue to our life, for example, without more.

How have we reached the point where we have such a poor understanding of how God acts in our life? How have we built such a legalistic religion, as if it were just a collection of practices that aim at nothing more than earning God's benevolence? Unfortunately, we are in great measure heirs to the early medieval philosophical current of nominalism. The nominalists aspired to save divine omnipotence and therefore held that the determination of what is just, good, or bad depends exclusively on an arbitrary decision by God, who establishes it as such, outside the reality of things. For example, if God had said it was licit to abandon or kill one's own parents, the nominalists would call that a good act. Basically, what they denied was the intrinsic goodness of created things. The sublime value of the theology of the creation, which holds that all of creation is an expression of God's goodness, was thereby nullified, and therefore justice was turned into the simple application of a norm. The final result was that mercy, as opposed to justice, carried with it an arbitrary decision by God to cancel just and deserved punishment.

In reality, God's justice is that which makes us just by his mercy, manifested in the crucified love of Christ's sacrifice on Golgotha. True, we did not deserve it, but, by God's pure generosity, his justice makes us just and holy if we embrace such a great gift. Mercy thereby becomes an internal facet of justice, the other side of the coin of divine goodness: God, by his merciful goodness, justifies us. By taking pity on us for our situation of sin and death, God treats us mercifully. From that we understand that there is no contradiction between mercy and justice but, rather, a mutual affinity between them.

Often, however, we identify mercy more with forgiveness, and we understand forgiveness as overcoming the punishment that justice would mete out to the sinner.

A final misunderstanding today consists in reducing mercy to the forgiveness of sins. It would be like an end-of-season sale, like a dispensation from divine law: to deal with the chronic reality of our misery and sin, mercy would consist of lowering the bar of what the Ten Commandments require.

I believe that God, as I said before, always takes us seriously. In his deeply heartfelt love for his creation, and especially for us, his children, he has enabled us to live in accordance with the sacraments and the moral life founded on them. By offering us his mercy, he has raised us up, and by raising us up, he has entirely transformed our existence: a person who has known Christ, who has truly embraced him, changes his habits, his relationships, his entire way of dealing with all of reality. As he goes through the experience of purification and forgiveness, he feels himself inspired to live, in a certain way, at God's level.

It would therefore be an impoverishment of God's mercy to see it the way the Protestants do, as a *favor Dei* or the mere nullification of our sins. God, in having mercy on us, would cover our sins, yes, but he would in reality be leaving us in the situation in which we were before: the only thing that would have changed would be God himself, who would no longer pay attention to our faults, while we would in fact go on unchanged from what we had been before.

In sound Catholic theology, the authentic forgiveness of sins is based on the sinner's passage from a state of sin and opposition to God, from a dark life without God, to the shining state of sanctifying grace, to full communion with him. A person who is forgiven undergoes a real and radical transformation: this is called "created grace". Such an act is not performed automatically, however, without relying on man's freedom. The Council of Trent taught *in merito* that in order for man to receive forgiveness and mercy, voluntary *susceptio* is necessary on his part, that is, acceptance of forgiveness through grace. Therefore, although the sinner may be dead to the life of grace because of his sin, he continues to function in his nature, his will, and his freedom, which may be transformed, purified, and raised up by God in order to make that acceptance possible.

Catholicism does not recognize the life of grace without the participation of the sinner, without his will to renew his life. We are God's co-workers. The greatness of the Christian life is always achieved under the hallmark of "synergy": God does everything he must do, and we for our part must do what we must do. This is the great mystery of grace, which does not destroy our nature or our freedom, and much less does it suspend our intelligence, instead favoring and making it possible for us to live up to our full potential. God's mercy also works that way: not by suspending what is human in us, but by actuating it fully.

Yet culturally, the preaching of mercy has drawn a very harsh crit-icism: Nietzsche considered that pity was degrading both to him who sought it and to him who granted it, precisely because it did not help address the drama of life, taking refuge in the easy solu-tion of a life that could always be reshaped. The great subject of mercy today meets with a radical cultural difficulty, which is that it is confused with compassion. In itself compassion can serve as a good beginning, and it is therefore a part of mercy. But the latter would seem to mean something more. Some identify mercy with patience, with the ability to embrace and wait for the other, even with tolerance. There is no doubt that patience is also an element of mercy. We nevertheless wonder whether Christian mercy means something more. The question would be: Can mercy truly change one's heart and life? Is it therefore more than simple compassion or patience? The recent concluding document of the Synod on the Family of 2015 sees conversion as part of mercy. Can God in his mercy cause man to live at his level, at God's level, and from there become a source of mercy?

First of all, we should approach the concept of compas-sion more carefully. All passion implies something passive that one suffers, so compassion would be something that I perceive passively, something that happens in me almost spontaneously, as a reaction to another person's misfor-tune. It would be like mere empathy with that person, a natural solidarity that sometimes happens. It would be something passive, and it would depend on my character. For example, if an advertisement for an NGO is shown in the intermission of a movie to solicit contributions for a good cause, I might or might not feel compassion, depending on the particular moment. If this happened just before Christmas, I might contribute at one of the many events that are organized to raise funds for charita-ble causes.

This compassion is good and praiseworthy, but God's mercy goes beyond that; his mercy is an "admirable exchange"; he calls us to participate in his love, which in itself is strength and a fully active dynamism. God's mercy is not limited to his affective identification with our suffering, but, instead, it truly transforms us, makes us new creatures, capable of loving with his same love.

Saint Paul expresses this very well when he says that God the Father made Jesus "to be sin" (see 2 Cor 5:21). It is not easy to understand this passage. What it means is that Jesus not only gave his life for us, as other good men might have done. There is something more in Christ: one can give one's own life for others without that gift having a truly soteriological, salvational value, without its being an "agent of salvation". One may give one's life out of compassion, but in Jesus we find much more, because unlike that good man, who could bring himself to give his life for a friend, Jesus became sin for our sake. This is what is known as the vicarious character of Christ's dedication: his death is a "vicarious sacrifice". Jesus has shouldered our sin and identified himself with it. This is the greatest possible act of mercy, which truly transforms its object, because in his solicitude for the object's good, he does not simply give him something superficial: Christ has actually destroyed sin. Sin died when he did. Through him, death has died. What an unsurpassable work of mercy!

In this sense, I believe that it would be a serious mistake to understand the current Year of Mercy as the "end-of-season sale" that I mentioned, as a kind of discounting of the requirements of the sacraments, the Christian life, the Decalogue, the commandments, the Beatitudes. The purpose of this Jubilee is to invite us to renew ourselves as followers of Christ, not to present a Christianity lite that is ultimately of no interest to anyone.

The Jubilee of Mercy must help us all avoid the false interpretation of mercy that the world so often presents to us. It continuously invites us to live in a perpetual state of adolescence, sometimes even in the very way we dress or behave, without taking on the great responsibilities of life—following our own whims, giving priority to our tastes, our moods, our achievements, our comfort ... and also, in case we might suffer some scruple of conscience, excusing and consoling us with the idea that "God always forgives."

It is true: God always forgives, but he forgives only the sinners who beg forgiveness, who recognize their sin. Heartfelt contrition is always necessary. Through this first human act under the guidance of grace, which involves also a "voluntary acceptance" of forgiveness, the person feels pain on account of the wrong he has committed and understands the responsibility that he has in his guilt. From that is born a serious and specific intent to change his life with the grace of God: it is what is called the "amends" or "satisfaction" or "penance" for sin, its "expiation". It would be very frivolous, and in fact a temptation of God, if we were to say what Voltaire said: "God is mercy, what can he do? He has no choice but to forgive."

A theologian has defined the Christian way as the step from "kyrie eleison" (from the prayer for forgiveness) to "be merciful, even as your Father [who is in heaven] is merciful" (when the Christian becomes a source of mercy). What does this vision imply? What is the concept of mercy behind it?

Saint Paul invited us to be imitators of God (see Eph 5:1). This involves imitating God in his mercy, which means taking a path for which we have received the dynamic force of the Holy Spirit, poured into our hearts (see Rom 5:5). This is a first important sign: mercy is a path to be followed by which God raises us up little by little so we can escape our selfishness and incorporate our neighbor in our life.

This gradual aspect of mercy does not signal a reduction of God's commandments. We know, for example, that marriage is indissoluble, that the union of a man and a woman has "forever" as an essential and unforsakable characteristic, and that spousal love is therefore so deep and so beautiful. So in a traumatic situation where a woman has been abandoned by her husband, in the context of a sacramental marriage, whether consummated or unconsummated, it would not be permissible to say "let us be merciful and allow her to contract a new marriage with another man." This would not be true mercy but, instead, a failure to take her personal travail seriously, besides favoring sin and mocking God and his commandments.

In fact, an act of mercy is not the equivalent of what we call a humanitarian act. Humanists, too, can be compassionate, but the Lord says, "Be merciful, even as your Father is merciful" (Lk 6:36). The key word is "as". What would seem to be an absurd attempt at equivalence with God becomes possible because he shares his own merciful love with us so that our hearts will be like his. Mercy belongs to revelation, to grace, to the eschatological presence of God in Jesus Christ, through whom we enter into our filial relationship with God.

We can understand true mercy and act on our understanding only through the eyes of faith, because another person, beyond simply being the object of my empathy or solidarity, is the same Jesus Christ who invites me to embrace him and include him in my life: "As you did it to one of the least of these my brethren, you did it to me"

(Mt 25:40). When I live mercy, I live the very life of God, and therefore, with the strength of the Holy Spirit, I can love the other as I do Christ, embracing him and including him in my life.

This means that mercy can only be understood in the context of a global vision that embraces the whole narrative of the person. One who does not see the entirety, the past, present, and future of the life of a person, can regard as mercy an act that actually is profoundly destructive, that becomes a dead-end street. What can truly help us attain a good understanding of mercy? How can we better understand that correction, teaching, and advising are also works of mercy?

Saying "no" to desires is sometimes a part of mercy. In the case of a drug addict or alcoholic, the truly merciful attitude prompts one to provide to the other, not more drugs or more alcohol, but instead the possibility of escaping from the dependence that dehumanizes him. When, for example, someone squanders his money or falls victim to the vice of gambling, the merciful thing to do is to help him escape from that situation, not to confirm him in it. Nor would it be a merciful reaction for a priest who, in order not to lose a member of the parish who is financially generous but very preoccupied with his business, to say, "Don't worry, don't be anxious; given how busy you are, you don't need to come to Mass on Sundays."

Mercy always seeks the good of the whole person, both his natural and his supernatural good. It therefore does not try to satisfy or justify irregular desires. Even less does it make itself complicit in a sin or omission when it is a matter of the fulfillment of the sinner's potential. It is what has been called in the tradition of the Church a "fraternal correction", one of the more complicated but most sublime forms of mercy. When a university student admits that he is leading a dissolute and vicious life, his parents cannot say to him, "Don't worry, we've known that you've been wasting your time and our money, but you know that you just need to pass your exams." To me, those parents, so mediocre as parents, would be ruining their child by keeping him from seeing the vocation to fulfillment to which he is called by God.

God is also demanding. He is a good father, and as such he asks us to develop our talents and capacities for our own good and that of others. He asks us to exert ourselves and be decisive in starting over after every tumble we might take as we make our way in life. His mercy never ignores or hides our responsibility.

Can we say that the family is God's first mercy toward man? In what sense?

The family, as an analogy to the Church, is a unique expression and privileged pathway of God's mercy. The Church is the place of divine mercy, the privileged space for experiencing it. The family, as the "domestic Church", makes possible the initial experiences of true mercy: it is in the family that one learns to forgive "seventy times seven" times (Mt 18:22)—that is, always. And it is there that we learn that the Christian name of God is "Father", because it is founded on a first basic experience of what the father-child relationship means. The supernatural life of grace, without these initial experiences, would be impossible: it is what the ancients call the *preambula fidei*—that is, what prepares and precedes the experience of faith.

Grace is always premised on nature and raises it up: especially the basic human experience of family life. That is the only way to understand that the family is the first expression of God's mercy toward us, something like a *preambula misericordiae*, where our future experience of divine mercy can be ensconced and developed.

"Proclaiming the truth in love is itself an act of mercy." This was one of the conclusions of the extraordinary Synod on the Family in 2014. What is your view of this sentence? Can we say that, in our "late-modern" context, this is really the greatest mercy?

I said before that mercy cannot consist in relativizing God's commandments but must, rather, make possible the encounter with God's love, which renews and changes our life. Mercy consists in recognizing that the truth, the truth of love, will make us free (see Jn 8:32). In that connection, I should make it clear that love and truth are not two elements that compete with each other, between which one must choose. What would love be without truth? It would be a purely transient feeling, a deceptive effect, perhaps more intense but sterile and the cause of great dissatisfaction. What would truth without love be? An arid affirmation that would never touch my life or my heart, that would not resonate with me.

We have to be very careful with the expression to which you are referring, so it will not be misunderstood or set off an ingenuous and superficial discussion. Let us suppose, for example, the case of a person who is responsible for genocide. In the context of such a case, what would it mean to "tell him the truth with love"? That expression could not be applied here without thoroughly qualifying it beforehand, because the truth requires also, in circumstances like these, a threat, legal proceedings, punishment, and even the reminder of trial before God, the certainty that he can condemn the sinner who does not repent.

Hell, certainly, is not just a rhetorical and pedagogical tool with which to frighten sinners: it is a real possibility. We often think about merely venial sins of everyday life, sins that are committed by respectable people. But what should we say about drug traffickers? And about people who trade in white slaves or immigrants? Can we possibly be silent when we are dealing with genocide? How do we deal with the actions of exploiters or terrorists? Should we refer euphemistically to cases of corruption among politicians? We cannot be so naïve as to think that cases like the ones I have just mentioned are very rare. We cannot preach a bourgeois version of mercy, thinking only of problems that arise in the context of the institution of marriage in Western countries, where, in the end, they are nothing more than debates about the little life of the bourgeois middle-class Western hedonist.

We have already said that modern man mistrusts mercy. What mercy can the Church offer him? Our contemporaries certainly seek forgiveness and mercy, but do they do so only to assuage a guilty feeling? What can we identify in this search?

Mercy as such is a reality that is intimately linked to the admission that God exists and is historically active among us. If that premise is granted, implementing it is not compatible with the objective of assuaging consciences. How can modern man find peace and reconciliation with himself? There is only one way open to us: compunction or repentance for the evil committed. The Cross of Christ is the only path. There is no other path for evangelization today.

In the Jewish tradition before Christ, we also find the Servant of God who suffers as a representative of the people, as a symbolic person. This figure is a good starting point for understanding the mercy that Jesus brings us: we know through Christ that any sin attains forgiveness if the sinner accepts God's forgiveness, if he humbles himself before him, if he adopts the same attitude that David did when he exclaimed, "Against you, you only, have I sinned" (Ps 51:4).

This crucial step does not depend on God alone; it also depends on the repentant sinner. What is more, the sinner's pain is not relieved immediately: the disorder caused in him and in his own relationships is not easily remedied. For example, imagine the criminal penalty that the guilty person must expiate before God and society: it is clear to everyone that the forgiveness of his sins does not directly imply relief from all his punishment. Forgiveness does not save the repentant criminal from still having to work hard, as hard as he can, to make amends for his sins by expunging or setting right their consequences. When his forgiveness has been accepted, God has restored his friendship, but the sinner is also fully conscious of the aftereffects and suffering that his sins have left behind them. This is a penalty that he has to purge in this life or in the next, through the mediation of the forgiveness that the Church performs. Because of this "temporal penalty", which is what it is called in order to differentiate it from the "eternal penalty" that is forgiven in absolution, the Church, from the merits of Christ and the saints, offers us all possible assistance in healing the wounds occasioned by the sin—more specifically, the assistance that we call the *indulgences*. These benign concessions in our favor are the great gift of every jubilee, such as this Year of Mercy. If we know how to avail ourselves of them, they can be a magnificent aid in repairing our relationship with God, with others, and with ourselves.

I see some very positive elements in the energetic, if tormented, search in which man is engaged today, and even in some guilt feelings, because they bespeak an implicit recognition of need. It is no more than a first step. It is not yet an experience of mercy. Only in the encounter with the living God, with all the requirements that entails, can that step be taken. The Church has a great role to play in taking it, because today's man, like the Samaritan woman who came upon Jesus by the well, needs to know that the true water exists that can slake his thirst (see Jn 4:1–42).

Before we close, I would like to consider the ultimate realities, the God who awaits us in eternal life. What is the relationship between the hopes we have discussed and the great hope, between life in the flesh and eternal life? If God's work of mercy is what causes his Spirit to live in our flesh and makes us children in his Son, this will be granted fully at the end, in eternal life. How should that prospect animate our lesser hopes? What does "eternal life" mean to Christian hope?

Eternal life, inchoate in this world, is our great hope. This trust sustains our lesser hopes, which are conditioned by our daily and earthly life. When a young man sets his hopes on the young woman whom he is getting to know at the beginning of their courtship, when he hopes to pass an exam that will enable him to pursue his studies, when a couple learn for the first time that they are expecting a child, there is a surge of hope that is like a beautiful tile in the great mosaic that depicts our life.

Eternal life is the great hope that guides the steps of each of us to their final destination. Often, it protects us against despair or the temptations of comfort and laziness. Sometimes, it enables us to surmount spiritual sadness, our routine, or a false resignation: conformism is nothing but the expression of a lack of hope in our lives.

Some might say that routine and conformism can turn hope into a "bourgeois virtue". I am thinking of moments when in our cowardice, to avoid complicating our lives, we avoid a confrontation, an exam, or a judgment. When we shy away from embracing people who are different from us. When we prefer to stay home watching television or to take an expensive trip as a way of escaping the distressing mediocrity of our life, instead of taking care of our elderly parents, spending more time with our children, or helping out in the parish. These are cases of a hope that is in great need of purification.

"'Blessed are the dead who from now on die in the Lord.' 'Blessed indeed,' says the Spirit, 'that they may rest from their labors, for their deeds follow them!'" (Rev 14:13): they are numbered among the blessed because they discover that nothing has been in vain, that none of their efforts was for naught. The certainty that we all must die, that this world is finite and its justice is always imperfect, leads us into a very deep wisdom, which is reserved, not for the academics and the learned, but rather for those simple people who know how to welcome God into their hearts. They are the ones who have understood life's great lesson: that everything is summed up in Christ. This is our great hope. The communion of saints, the body of which Christ is the head, is our ultimate hope, because he will come, so that at the end all will be all in God: "When all things are subjected to him, then the Son himself will also be subjected to him who put all things under him, that God may be everything to every one" (1 Cor 15:28).